COLLINS GEM

French
PHRASE FINDER

HarperCollins*Publishers*

CONSULTANT
Josiane Nicolas

OTHER GEM PHRASE FINDERS

DUTCH
GERMAN
GREEK
ITALIAN
PORTUGUESE
SPANISH

book and tape packs:

French
German
Italian
Spanish

First published 1993
Copyright © HarperCollins Publishers
Reprint 10 9 8 7 6 5 4
Printed in Great Britain

ISBN 0 00-470285-9

BUSINESS

- ACCOUNTS
- BUSINESS—MEETING
- COMPUTERS
- FAX
- IMPORT/EXPORT
- LETTERS
- OFFICE
- WORK

TRAVEL

- see **CAR**
- AIR TRAVEL
- BOAT, FERRY...
- BUS
- CUSTOMS CONTROL
- METRO
- TAXI
- TRAIN

EATING & DRINKING

- DRINKING
- EATING OUT
- VEGETARIAN
- WINES & SPIRITS

CAR

- BREAKDOWNS
- CAR—DRIVING
- CAR—HIRE
- CAR—PARTS
- PETROL STATION

DIFFICULTIES

- COMPLAINTS
- EMERGENCIES
- PROBLEMS

LEISURE

- CELEBRATIONS
- CINEMA
- ENTERTAINMENT
- LEISURE/INTERESTS
- MUSIC
- SIGHTSEEING & TOURIST OFFICE
- SKIING
- SPORTS
- TELEVISION
- THEATRE
- WALKING

SHOPPING

- CLOTHES
- FOOD—GENERAL, FRUIT & VEG.
- MAPS, GUIDES & NEWSPAPERS
- PHARMACY
- PHOTOS & VIDEOS
- POST OFFICE
- SHOPPING—SHOPS
- STATIONERY

ACCOMMODATION

- ACCOMMODATION
- CAMPING
- DISABLED TRAVELLERS
- HOTEL
- ROOM SERVICE
- SIGHTSEEING & TOURIST OFFICE

PRACTICALITIES

- ALPHABET
- BASICS
- COLOUR & SHAPE
- DAYS, MONTHS & SEASONS
- DIRECTIONS
- LAUNDRY
- LUGGAGE
- MEASUREMENTS & QUANTITIES
- MONEY
- NUMBERS
- PAYING
- QUESTIONS
- REPAIRS
- SIGNS & NOTICES
- TELEPHONE
- TIME—TIME PHRASES

HEALTH

- BODY
- DENTIST
- DOCTOR
- EMERGENCIES
- PHARMACY

MEETING PEOPLE

- BASICS
- CELEBRATIONS
- GREETINGS
- MAKING FRIENDS
- WORK
- WEATHER

Your *Collins Gem Phrase Finder* is designed to help you locate the exact phrase you need in any situation, whether for holiday or business. If you want to adapt the phrases, we have made sure that you can easily see where to substitute your own words (you can find them in the dictionary section), and the clear, alphabetical, two-colour layout gives you direct access to the different topics.

The *Phrase Finder* includes:

- Over 70 topics arranged alphabetically from **ACCOMMODATION** to **WORK**. Each phrase is accompanied by a simple pronunciation guide which ensures that there's no problem over pronouncing the foreign words.

- Practical hints and useful vocabulary highlighted in boxes. Where the English words appear first in the box, this indicates vocabulary you may need. Where the red French words appear first, these are words you are more likely to see written on signs and notices.

WORDS APPEARING IN BLACK ARE ENGLISH WORDS	WORDS APPEARING IN RED ARE FRENCH WORDS

- Possible phrases you may hear in reply to your questions. The foreign phrases appear in red.

- A clearly laid-out 5000-word dictionary: English words in black and French words appear in red.

- A basic grammar section which will enable you to build on your phrases.

It's worth spending time before you embark on your travels just looking through the topics to see what is covered and becoming familiar with what might be said to you.

Whatever the situation, your *Phrase Finder* is sure to help!

CONTENTS

LIST OF TOPICS

PRONOUNCING FRENCH ——————— ENGLISH-FRENCH

In this book we have used a simple system to help you pronounce the phrases. We have designed the book so that as you read the pronunciation of the phrases you can follow the French. This will help you to recognize the different sounds and enable you to read French without relying on the guide. Here are a few rules you should know:

FRENCH	SOUNDS LIKE	EXAMPLE	PRONUNCIATION
■ É	ay	été	aytay
■ È	eh	très	treh
■ C (+ A, O, U)	ka, ko, ku	cas, col, cur	ka, kol, koor
■ C (+ E, I), ç	s	ceci, leçon	suhsee, luhsoñ
■ CH	sh	chat	sha
■ EU	uh	neuf	nuhf
■ EAU	oh	beau	boh
■ U	oo	sur	soor
■ G (+ E, I)	zhe, zhee	gel, gîte	zhel, zheet
■ GN	ny	saignant	say-nyoñ
■ OI	wa	roi	rwa
■ UI	wee	huit	weet

*E is sometimes weak and sounds like **uh**. This happens either in very short words **je** zhuh, **le** luh, **se** suh, etc., or when the E falls at the end of a syllable:*
retard ruhtar, **demain** duhmañ.

H is not pronounced: **hôtel** ohtel, **homard** omar.

*There are nasal vowels in French (represented by **ñ**):*
un uñ, **fin** fañ, **on** oñ, **dans** doñ, **bain** bañ, **en** oñ.

Final consonants are often silent: **Paris** pa-ree, **Londres** loñdr. *However, sometimes the ending is pronounced if it is followed by a word which begins with a vowel:*
avez-vous avay voo **but vous avez** vooz avay.

■ ALPHABET

6

If you haven't booked your accommodation, check with the local tourist office to see if they have a list of hotels and guesthouses.

HÔTEL	HOTEL	COMPLET	FULL
CHAMBRES	ROOMS AVAILABLE	PENSION	GUESTHOUSE

Do you have a list of accommodation with prices?
Est-ce que vous avez une liste des hôtels avec les prix?
es kuh vooz avay oon leest dayz ohtel avek lay pree

Is there a hotel here?
Il y a un hôtel ici?
eel ya uñ ohtel eesee

Do you have any vacancies?
Vous avez des chambres?
vooz avez day shoñbr

I'd like (to book) a room...
Je voudrais (réserver) une chambre...
zhuh voodray (rayzehr-vay) oon shoñbr...

double
pour deux personnes
poor duh pehr-son

single
pour une personne
poor oon pehr-son

with bath
avec bain
avek bañ

with shower
avec douche
avek doosh

with a double bed
à un lit
a uñ lee

twin-bedded
à deux lits
a duh lee

with an extra bed for a child
avec un autre lit pour un enfant
avek uñ ohtr lee poor uñ oñfoñ

A quiet room that looks onto...
Une chambre tranquille qui donne sur...
oon shoñbr troñkeel kee don soor...

the back
la cour
la koor

the sea
la mer
la mehr

We'd like two rooms next to each other
On voudrait deux chambres l'une à côté de l'autre
oñ voodray duh shoñbr loon a kotay duh lohtr

We'd like to stay ... nights
On voudrait rester ... nuits
oñ voodray restay ... nwee

from ... till ...
du ... au ...
doo ... oh ...

CONT...

I will confirm...
Je confirmerai...
zhuh koñfeerm-ray...

by letter
par lettre
par letr

by fax
par fax
par fax

How much is it...?
C'est combien...?
say koñ-byañ...

per night
par nuit
par nwee

per week
par semaine
par smen

How much is...?
C'est combien...?
say koñ-byañ...

half board
la demi-pension
la duhmee poñ-syoñ

full board
la pension
la poñ-syoñ

Have you anything cheaper?
Avez-vous quelque chose de moins cher?
avay voo kelkuh shohz duh mwañ shehr

Are there any other hotels nearby?
Il y a d'autres hôtels dans le coin?
eel ya dohtre ohtel doñ luh kwañ

■ **YOU MAY HEAR**

C'est complet
say koñpleh
We're full up

C'est pour combien de nuits?
say poor koñ-byañ duh nwee
For how many nights?

C'est pour combien de personnes?
say poor koñ-byañ duh pehr-son
For how many people?

Votre nom, s'il vous plaît?
votr noñ seel voo pleh
Your name, please?

Veuillez confirmer...
vuh-yay koñfeermay...
Please confirm...

par lettre
par letr
by letter

par fax
par fax
by fax

■ CAMPING ■ HOTEL ■ SIGHTSEEING & TOURIST OFFICE

ACCOUNTANT	LE/LA COMPTABLE
AN INVOICE	UNE FACTURE
TO SETTLE (to pay)	RÉGLER

I'd like to speak to someone in your accounts department
Je voudrais parler à quelqu'un dans votre service de comptabilité
zhuh voodray parlay a kelkuñ doñ votr sehrvees duh coñtabeelee-tay

It's regarding invoice number...
C'est au sujet de la facture numéro...
say oh soozheh duh la fak-toor noomayro...

I think there is an error
Je pense qu'il y a une erreur
zhuh poñs keel ya oon eh-rur

We are still waiting for the invoice to be settled
Nous attendons toujours le règlement de la facture
nooz atoñdoñ toozhoor luh rehgluhmoñ duh la fak-toor

Please supply a credit note and new invoice
Veuillez nous envoyer un avoir et une nouvelle facture
vuh-yay nooz oñvwa-yay uñ avwar ay oon noovel fak-toor

Please address the invoice to...
Veuillez adresser la facture à...
vuh-yay adressay la fak-toor à...

Please state content and value of the consignment
Veuillez déclarer le contenu et la valeur de l'envoi
vuh-yay daykla-ray luh koñtuhnoo ay la va-lur duh loñvwa

■ YOU MAY HEAR

Nous voulons un règlement à 30/60 jours fin de mois
noo vooloñ uñ raygl-moñ a troñt/swasoñt zhoor fañ duh mwa
Payment is 30/60 days from end of month of receipt of invoice

■ NUMBERS ■ TELEPHONE

9

Most signs are in French and English and you may go through the airport without having to speak any French. Here are a few signs you will find useful to know. The blue customs channel is for EC citizens travelling within Europe who have no goods to declare.

ARRIVÉES	**ARRIVALS**
CONTRÔLE DE PASSEPORTS	**PASSPORT CONTROL**
PASSEPORTS CE	**EC PASSPORT HOLDERS**
AUTRES PASSEPORTS	**OTHER PASSPORTS**
RETRAIT DES BAGAGES	**BAGGAGE RECLAIM**
DOUANE	**CUSTOMS CONTROL**
RIEN À DÉCLARER	**NOTHING TO DECLARE**
ARTICLES À DÉCLARER	**ARTICLES TO DECLARE**
RENSEIGNEMENTS	**INFORMATION**
SORTIE	**EXIT**
NAVETTE	**AIRPORT BUS : SHUTTLE SERVICE**

Where is the luggage for the flight from...?
Où sont les bagages du vol en provenance de...?
oo soñ lay bagazh doo vol oñ provnoñs duh...

Where can I change some money?
Où est-ce que je peux changer de l'argent?
oo es kuh zhuh puh shoñzhay duh la-rzhoñ

How do I/we get into town?
Pour aller en ville?
poor alay oñ veel

How much is the taxi fare...? into town to the hotel
C'est combien le taxi pour aller...? en ville à l'hôtel
say koñ-byañ luh taxi poor alay... *oñ veel* *a lohtel*

Is there an airport bus to the city centre?
Est-ce qu'il y a une navette pour aller au centre-ville?
es keel ya oon navet poor alay oh soñtr veel

■ BUS ■ LUGGAGE ■ METRO ■ TAXI

DÉPARTS	DEPARTURES		
INTERNATIONAUX	INTERNATIONAL	DOMESTIQUES	NATIONAL
CARTE D'EMBARQUEMENT	BOARDING CARD	VOL	FLIGHT
PORTE NUMÉRO...	GATE NUMBER...	RETARD	DELAY

Where do I check in for flight ... to...?
Où est-ce qu'il faut enregistrer pour le vol ... à destination de...?
oo es keel foh oñruh-zheestray poor luh vol ... a desteena-syoñ duh...

Which is the departure gate for the flight to...?
Quelle est la porte d'embarquement pour le vol à destination de...? *kel eh la port doñbahrk-moñ poor luh vol a desteena-syoñ duh...*

■ YOU MAY HEAR

L'embarquement aura lieu à la porte numéro...
loñbark-moñ ohra lyuh a la port noomayro...
Boarding will take place at gate number...

Présentez-vous immédiatement à la porte numéro...
prayzoñtay voo eemay-dyat-moñ a la port noomayro...
Go immediately to gate number...

Votre vol a du retard
votr vol a doo ruhtar
Your flight is delayed

■ IF YOU NEED TO CHANGE OR CHECK ON YOUR FLIGHT

I want to change / cancel my reservation
Je voudrais changer / annuler ma réservation
zhuh voodray shoñ-zhay / anoolay ma rayzehrva-syoñ

I'd like to reconfirm my flight to...
Je voudrais confirmer mon vol pour...
zhuh voodray koñfeermay mon vol poor...

Is the flight to ... delayed?
Est-ce que le vol à destination de ... a du retard?
es kuh luh vol a desteena-syoñ duh ... a doo ruhtar

The French alphabet is the same as the English. Below are the words used for clarification when spelling something out.

How do you spell it?
Comment ça s'écrit?
komoñ sa say-kree

A as in Anatole, b as in Berthe
A comme Anatole, b comme Berthe
a kom ana-tol bay kom behrt

A	*a*	**Anatole**	*ana-tol*
B	*bay*	**Berthe**	*behrt*
C	*say*	**Célestin**	*sayles-tañ*
D	*day*	**Désiré**	*dayzee-ray*
E	*uh*	**Eugène**	*uh-zhen*
F	*ef*	**François**	*froñswah*
G	*zhay*	**Gaston**	*gastoñ*
H	*ash*	**Henri**	*oñree*
I	*ee*	**Irma**	*eerma*
J	*zhee*	**Joseph**	*zhohzef*
K	*ka*	**Kléber**	*klaybehr*
L	*el*	**Louis**	*loo-ee*
M	*em*	**Marcel**	*marsel*
N	*en*	**Nicolas**	*neekoh-la*
O	*oh*	**Oscar**	*oskar*
P	*pay*	**Pierre**	*pyehr*
Q	*koo*	**Quintal**	*kañtal*
R	*ehr*	**Raoul**	*ra-ool*
S	*es*	**Suzanne**	*soozan*
T	*tay*	**Thérèse**	*tayrez*
U	*oo*	**Ursule**	*oorsool*
V	*vay*	**Victor**	*veektor*
W	*doo-bluh-vay*	**William**	*weel-yam*
X	*eex*	**Xavier**	*za-vyay*
Y	*ee grek*	**Yvonne**	*eevon*
Z	*zed*	**Zoé**	*zoh-ay*

Yes
Oui
wee

No
Non
noñ

OK!
Bien!
byañ

Please
S'il vous plaît
seel voo pleh

Don't mention it
De rien
duh ryañ

With pleasure!
Avec plaisir!
avek playzeer

Thank you
Merci
mehrsee

Thanks very much
Merci beaucoup
mehrsee bohkoo

Thanks, that's very kind
Merci, c'est gentil
mehrsee say zhoñtee

Sir / Mr
Monsieur / M.
muhsyuh

Madam / Mrs / Ms
Madame / Mme
madam

Miss
Mademoiselle / Mlle
mad-mwa-zel

Excuse me! *(to catch attention)*
Pardon, monsieur / madame
pardoñ muhsyuh / madam

Excuse me *(sorry)*
Excusez-moi
ekskoo-zay mwo

Pardon?
Comment?
komoñ

I don't know
Je ne sais pas
zhuh nuh seh pa

I don't understand
Je ne comprends pas
zhuh nuh koñproñ pa

Do you understand?
Vous comprenez?
voo koñpruhnay

Do you speak English?
Vous parlez anglais?
voo parlay oñgleh

I speak very little French
Je parle très peu le français
zhuh parl treh puh luh froñsay

Could you repeat that, please?
Pourriez-vous répéter, s'il vous plaît?
pooree-ay voo raypay-tay seel voo pleh

It's not serious
Ce n'est pas grave
snay pa grav

It doesn't matter
Ça ne fait rien
sanuh feh ryañ

When is the next boat / hovercraft to...?
À quelle heure part le prochain bateau / aéroglisseur pour...?
a kel ur par luh proshañ batoh / a-ehro-glee-sur poor...

Have you a timetable?
Vous avez un horaire?
vooz avay uñ orehr

Is there a car ferry to...?
Est-ce qu'il y a un car ferry pour...?
es keel ya uñ car ferry poor...

How much is...?
C'est combien...?
seh koñ-byañ...?

a single
un aller simple
uñ alay sañpl

a return
un aller et retour
uñ alay ay ruhtoor

A tourist ticket
Un billet touristique
uñ bee-yay toorees-teek

How much is it for a car and ... people?
C'est combien pour une voiture et ... personnes?
say koñ-byañ poor oon vwatoor ay ... pehr-son

How long is the crossing?
La traversée dure combien de temps?
la travehrsay door koñ-byañ duh toñ

Where does the boat leave from?
D'où part le bateau?
doo par luh batoh

When is the first / last boat?
Le premier / dernier bateau part quand?
luh pruhm-yay / luh dehr-nyay batoh par koñ

What time do we get to...?
On arrive à quelle heure à...?
oñ a-reev a kel ur a...

Is there somewhere to eat on the boat?
Est-ce qu'on peut manger sur le bateau?
es koñ puh moñ-zhay soor luh batoh

14

In French the possessive (my, his, her, etc.) is generally not used with parts of the body, e.g.

I've broken my leg   *Je me suis cassé la jambe*
He's hurt his ankle   *Il s'est fait mal à la cheville*

ankle	la cheville	shuhveey
arm	le bras	bra
back	le dos	doh
bone	l'os	os
chin	le menton	moñtoñ
ear	l'oreille	o-ray
elbow	le coude	kood
eye, eyes	l'œil, les yeux	uhy, yuh
finger	le doigt	dwa
foot	le pied	pyay
hair	les cheveux	shuhvuh
hand	la main	mañ
head	la tête	tet
heart	le cœur	kur
hip	la hanche	oñsh
joint	l'articulation	artee-koola-syoñ
kidney	le rein	rañ
knee	le genou	zhuhnoo
leg	la jambe	zhoñb
liver	le foie	fwa
mouth	la bouche	boosh
nail	l'ongle	oñgl
nape of neck	la nuque	nook
nose	le nez	nay
stomach	l'estomac	esto-ma
throat	la gorge	gorzh
thumb	le pouce	poos
toe	l'orteil	ortay
wrist	le poignet	pwa-nyay

■ DOCTOR ■ PHARMACY

ASSISTANCE AUTOMOBILE	FRENCH EQUIVALENT TO AA

Can you help me?
Pouvez-vous m'aider?
poovay voo mayday

My car has broken down
Ma voiture est en panne
ma vwatoor eh oñ pan

I can't start the car
Je n'arrive pas à démarrer la voiture
zhuh na-reev pa a dayma-ray la vwatoor

The battery is flat
La batterie est à plat
la batree eh a pla

I've run out of petrol
Je suis en panne d'essence
zhuh swee oñ pan dessoñs

Is there a garage near here?
Il y a un garage près d'ici?
eel ya uñ garazh preh deesee

The engine's overheating
Le moteur chauffe
luh motur shohf

I need water
Il me faut de l'eau
eel muh foh duh loh

There's a leak
Il y a une fuite
eel ya oon fweet

I've a flat tyre
J'ai un pneu de crevé
zhay uñ pnuh duh kruhvay

I can't get the wheel off
Je ne peux pas démonter la roue
zhuh nuh puh pa daymoñtay la roo

Can you tow me to the nearest garage?
Pouvez-vous me remorquer jusqu'au garage le plus proche?
poovay voo muh ruhmor-kay zhooskoh garazh luh ploo prosh

Do you have parts for a (make of car)**...?**
Avez-vous des pièces de rechange pour une...?
avay voo day pyes duh ruhshoñzh poor oon...

There's something wrong with the... (see CAR–PARTS)
J'ai un problème avec le/la/les...
zhay uñ problem avek luh/la/lay...

Can you replace the windscreen?
Pouvez-vous remplacer le pare-brise?
poovay voo roñplasay luh parbreez

■ **CAR–PARTS**

BUS TICKET	UN TICKET DE BUS
BOOK OF TICKETS	UN CARNET DE TICKETS
TO GET ON THE BUS	MONTER DANS LE BUS
TO GET OFF THE BUS	DESCENDRE DU BUS

Is there a bus to...?
Est-ce qu'il y a un bus pour...?
es keel ya uñ boos poor...

Which route is it?
C'est quelle ligne?
say kel lee-nyuh

Where do I catch the bus to go to...?
Où est-ce qu'on prend le bus pour aller à/au (etc.)...?
oo es koñ proñ l-boos poor alay a/oh...?

Where can I buy bus tickets?
Où est-ce que je peux acheter des tickets de bus?
oo es kuh zhuh puh ashtay day teekay d-boos

How much is it to...?
C'est combien pour aller à/au (etc.)...?
say koñ-byañ poor alay a/oh...

to the centre
au centre
oh soñtr

to the beach
à la plage
a la plazh

to the shops
aux magasins
oh maga-zañ

to Montmartre
à Montmartre
a moñmartr

How often are the buses to...?
Les bus pour ... passent tous les combien?
lay boos poor ... pass too lay koñ-byañ

When is the first / the last bus to...?
À quelle heure part le premier / le dernier bus pour...?
a kel ur par luh pruhm-yay / luh dehr-nyay boos poor...

Please tell me when to get off
S'il vous plaît, vous me direz quand je dois descendre
seel voo pleh voo muh deeray koñ zhuh dwa dessoñdr

Please let me off
Arrêtez, s'il vous plaît
areh-tay seel voo pleh

This is my stop
C'est mon arrêt
say moñ areh

■ **METRO** ■ **TAXI**

BOARD MEETING	LA RÉUNION DU CONSEIL (D'ADMINISTRATION)
CONFERENCE ROOM	LA SALLE DE RÉUNION
MANAGING DIRECTOR	LE DIRECTEUR GÉNÉRAL
MEETING	LA RÉUNION
MINUTES	LE COMPTE RENDU
SAMPLE	UN ÉCHANTILLON
TO CHAIR A MEETING	PRÉSIDER LA RÉUNION
TO DRAW UP A CONTRACT	DRESSER UN CONTRAT
TRADE FAIR	LA FOIRE COMMERCIALE
TURNOVER	LE CHIFFRE D'AFFAIRES

I'd like to arrange a meeting with...
J'aimerais fixer une réunion avec...
zhem-ray feeksay oon ray-oon-yoñ avek...

Are you free to meet...?
Êtes-vous libre pour rencontrer...?
eht voo leebr poor roñkoñtray...

on the 4th May at 1100
le 4 mai à 11 heures
luh katr may a oñz ur

for breakfast
pour le petit déjeuner
poor luh puhtee dayzhuh-nay

for lunch
pour le déjeuner
poor luh dayzhuh-nay

for dinner
pour le dîner
poor luh deenay

I will confirm...
Je confirmerai...
zhuh koñfeerm-ray...

by letter
par lettre
par letr

by fax
par fax
par fax

I'm staying at Hotel...
Je suis à l'Hôtel...
zhuh swee a lohtel...

How do I get to your office?
Pour aller à votre bureau?
poor alay a votr boo-roh

Please let ... know that I will be ... minutes late
Veuillez faire savoir à ... que je serai en retard de ... minutes
vuh-yay fehr savvar a ... ke zhuh suh-ray oñ ruhtar duh ... meenoot

I have an appointment with...
J'ai rendez-vous avec ...
zhay roñday-voo avek ...

at ... o'clock
à ... heures
a ... ur

Here is my card
Voici ma carte de visite
vwasee ma kart duh veezeet

I'm delighted to meet you at last!
Je suis enchanté(e) de faire enfin votre connaissance!
zhuh swee oñshoñtay duh fehr oñfañ votr koneh-soñs

My French isn't very good
Mon français n'est pas très bon
moñ froñseh nay pa treh boñ

Please speak slowly
S'il vous plaît, parlez lentement
seel voo pleh parlay loñt-moñ

I'm sorry I'm late
Je suis désolé(e), je suis en retard
zhuh swee dayzo-lay zhuh swee oñ ruhtar

My flight was delayed
Mon vol avait du retard
moñ vol aveh doo ruhtar

May I introduce you to...
Je voudrais vous présenter à...
zhuh voodray voo prayzoñtay a...

Can I offer you dinner?
Est-ce que je peux vous inviter à dîner?
es kuh zhuh puh vooz añveetay a deenay

■ YOU MAY HEAR

Est-ce que vous avez rendez-vous?
es kuh vooz avay roñday-voo
Do you have an appointment?

...n'est pas dans le bureau
...neh pa doñ luh booroh
...isn't in the office

Il / Elle sera de retour dans cinq minutes
eel / el suh-ra doñ ruhtoor doñ sañk meenoot
He / She will be back in five minutes

■ FAX ■ LETTERS ■ OFFICE ■ TELEPHONE

19

ORDURES	RUBBISH
EAU POTABLE	DRINKING WATER
BLOC SANITAIRE	WASHING FACILITIES

Do you have a list of campsites with prices?
Avez-vous un guide des campings avec les prix?
avay voo uñ geed day koñpeeng avek lay pree

Is the campsite sheltered?
Est-ce que le camping est abrité?
es kuh luh koñpeeng eh abreetay

Is the beach far?
C'est loin la plage?
say lwañ la plazh

Is there a restaurant on the campsite?
Y a-t-il un restaurant dans le camping?
ee a-teel uñ resto-roñ doñ luh koñpeeng

Do you have any vacancies?
Est-ce que vous avez des emplacements de libre?
es kuh vooz avay dayz oñplas-moñ d-leebr

Does the price include...?
Est-ce que le prix comprend...?
es kuh luh pree koñproñ...

hot water
l'eau chaude
loh shohd

electricity
l'électricité
laylek-treeseetay

We'd like to stay for ... nights
Nous voudrions rester ... nuits
noo voodryoñ restay ... nwee

How much is it per night...?
C'est combien la nuit...?
say koñ-byañ la nwee...

for a tent
pour une tente
poor oon toñt

for a caravan
pour une caravane
poor oon karavan

Can I/we camp here overnight?
Est-ce qu'on pourrait camper ici cette nuit?
es koñ pooray koñpay eesee set nwee

■ SIGHTSEEING & TOURIST OFFICE

20

*Don't park in a **zone d'enlèvement** – your car will be towed away!*

ALLUMEZ VOS PHARES	SWITCH ON HEADLIGHTS
AUTOROUTE	MOTORWAY *(signs are in blue)*
CENTRE-VILLE	CITY CENTRE
CÉDEZ LE PASSAGE	GIVE WAY
DÉVIATION	DIVERSION
PÉAGE	TOLL FOR MOTORWAY
POIDS LOURDS	HEAVY VEHICLES
PRIORITÉ À DROITE	GIVE WAY TO VEHICLES FROM RIGHT
RALENTIR	SLOW DOWN
ROULEZ AU PAS	DEAD SLOW
SENS UNIQUE	ONE WAY
STATIONNEMENT INTERDIT	NO PARKING
TOUTES DIRECTIONS	ALL ROUTES
VIRAGE DANGEREUX	DANGEROUS BEND
VITESSE LIMITÉE	SPEED LIMIT

Can I/we park here?
On peut se garer ici?
oñ puh suh garay eesee

Do I/we need a parking disk?
Il faut un disque de stationnement?
eel foh uñ deesk duh stasyoñ-moñ

How long can I/we park for?
Combien de temps on peut se garer?
koñ-byañ duh toñ oñ puh suh garay

We're going to....
Nous allons à...
nooz aloñ a...

What's the best route?
Quelle est la meilleure route?
kel eh la may-yur root

Will the motorway be busy?
Est-ce qu'il y aura beaucoup de circulation sur l'autoroute?
es keel ee ohra bohkoo duh seerkoola-syoñ soor lohtoh-root

Is the pass open?
Est-ce que le col est ouvert?
es kuh luh kol eh oovehr

■ **BREAKDOWNS** ■ **PETROL STATION**

DRIVING LICENCE	LE PERMIS DE CONDUIRE
FULLY COMPREHENSIVE INSURANCE	L'ASSURANCE TOUS-RISQUES
REVERSE GEAR	LA MARCHE ARRIÈRE

I want to hire a car   **for...days**   **for the weekend**
Je voudrais louer une voiture pour...jours   pour le weekend
zhuh voodray looay oon vwatoor   *poor...zhoor*   *pour luh weekend*

What are your rates...?   **per day**   **per week**
Quels sont vos tarifs...?   par jour   par semaine
kel soñ voh tareef...   *par zhoor*   *par smen*

How much is the deposit?
Combien d'arrhes faut-il verser?
koñ-byañ dar foht eel vehrsay

Is there a mileage (kilometre) charge?   **How much is it?**
Est-ce que le kilométrage est en plus?   C'est combien?
es kuh luh keelo-maytrazh eh oñ ploos   *say koñ-byañ*

Does the price include fully comprehensive insurance?
Est-ce que le prix comprend l'assurance tous-risques?
es kuh luh pree koñproñ lasoo-roñs too reesk

Must I return the car here?   **By what time?**
Est-ce que je dois rendre la voiture ici?   Vers quelle heure?
es kuh zhuh dwa roñdr la vwatoor eesee   *vehr kel ur*

I'd like to leave it in...
Je voudrais la laisser à...
zhuh voodray la lay-say a...

How do the controls work?
Pouvez-vous me montrer les commandes?
poovay voo muh moñtray lay komoñd

■ **YOU MAY HEAR**

Veuillez rendre la voiture avec un plein d'essence
vuh-yay roñdr la vwatoor avek uñ plañ dessoñs
Please return the car with a full tank

The ... doesn't work	**The ... don't work**
Le/La/L' ... ne marche pas	Les ... ne marchent pas
luh/la/l ... nuh marsh pa	lay ... nuh marsh pa

accelerator	l'accélérateur	aksay-layra-tur
battery	la batterie	batree
bonnet	le capot	kapo
brakes	les freins	frañ
choke	le starter	starter
clutch	l'embrayage	oñbray-yazh
dipped beam	(se mettre) en code	(suh metr) oñ kod
distributor	le delco	delko
engine	le moteur	motur
exhaust pipe	le pot d'échappement	poh dayshap-moñ
fuse	le fusible	foo-zeebl
gears	les vitesses	veetess
handbrake	le frein à main	frañ a mañ
headlights	les phares	far
ignition	l'allumage	aloo-mazh
indicator	le clignotant	klee-nyotoñ
points	les vis platinées	vees platee-nay
radiator	le radiateur	radya-tur
reversing lights	les phares de recul	far d-ruhkool
seat belt	la ceinture de sécurité	sañtoor d-saykooreetay
spare wheel	la roue de secours	roo d-suhkoor
spark plugs	les bougies	boo-zhee
steering	la direction	deerek-syoñ
steering wheel	le volant	voloñ
tyre	le pneu	pnuh
wheel	la roue	roo
windscreen	le pare-brise	parbreez
--washers	le lave-glace	lavglas
-- wiper	l'essuie-glace	eswee-glas

■ BREAKDOWNS ■ PETROL STATION

23

I'd like to wish you a...
Je vous souhaite un/une...
zhuh voo soo-ayt uñ/oon...

Merry Christmas!
Joyeux Noël!
zhwa-yuh noel

Happy New Year!
Bonne et Heureuse Année!
bon ay uruhz anay

Happy Easter!
Joyeuses Pâques!
zhwa-yuz pak

Happy (Saint's) Name Day!
Bonne Fête!
bon feht

Happy birthday!
Bon anniversaire!
bon anee-vehrsehr

Have a good trip!
Bon voyage!
bon vwa-yazh

Best wishes!
Meilleurs voeux!
may-yur vuh

Welcome!
Bienvenue!
byañ-vuhnoo

Enjoy your meal!
Bon appétit!
bon apaytee

Thanks, and the same to you!
Merci, à vous aussi!
mehrsee a vooz ohsee

Your health!
À votre santé!
a votr soñtay

Cheers!
À la vôtre!
a la votr

Congratulations!
Félicitations!
faylee-seeta-syoñ

■ LETTERS ■ MAKING FRIENDS

INTERDIT AUX MOINS DE 13/18 ANS	FORBIDDEN TO PERSONS UNDER 13/18
AVEC DES SOUS-TITRES	WITH SUB-TITLES
LA SÉANCE	PERFORMANCE
VO (version originale)	ORIGINAL VERSION

What's on at the cinema?
Qu'est-ce qu'il passe au cinéma?
kes keel pass oh seenay-ma

When does the film start / finish?
Le film commence / finit à quelle heure?
luh feelm komoñs / feenee a kel ur

Is it dubbed or subtitled?
Est-ce qu'il est doublé ou sous-titré?
es keel eh dooblay oo soo-teetray

How much are the tickets?
C'est combien les billets?
say koñ-byañ lay bee-yay

I'd like two seats at ... francs
Je voudrais deux places à ... francs
zhuh voodray duh plas a ... froñ

What films have you seen recently?
Quels films avez-vous vus récemment?
kel feelm avay voo voo ray-semoñ

What is (English name of film) called in French?
Comment est-ce que ... s'appelle en français?
komoñ es kuh ... sapel oñ froñseh

Who is your favourite actor?
Quel est votre acteur préféré?
kel eh votr aktur prayfay-ray

Who is your favourite actress?
Quelle est votre actrice préférée?
kel eh votr aktrees prayfay-ray

■ ENTERTAINMENT ■ LEISURE/INTERESTS

*Size for clothes is **la taille**. Size for shoes is **la pointure***

women		men - suits		shoes			
sizes		**sizes**		**sizes**			
UK	EC	UK	EC	UK	EC	UK	EC
10	36	36	46	2	35	8	42
12	38	38	48	3	36	9	43
14	40	40	50	4	37	10	44
16	42	42	52	5	38	11	45
18	44	44	54	6	39		
20	46	46	56	7	41		

May I try this on?
Est-ce que je peux l'essayer?
es kuh zhuh puh leh-say-yay

Where are the changing rooms?
Où sont les cabines d'essayage?
oo soñ lay kabeen dessay-yazh

Do you have it...?
L'avez-vous...?
lavay voo...

in a bigger size
en plus grand
oñ ploo groñ

in a smaller size
en plus petit
oñ ploo puhtee

Do you have this in any other colours?
Est-ce que vous l'avez dans d'autres coloris?
es kuh voo lavay doñ dohtr koloree

That's a shame!
C'est dommage!
say domazh

It's...
Il est...
eel eh...

too short
trop court
troh koor

too long
trop long
troh loñ

I'm just looking
Je regarde seulement
zhuh ruhgard suhlmoñ

I'll take it
Je le prends
zhuh luh proñ

■ **YOU MAY HEAR**

Quelle est votre taille?
kel eh votr tye
What size (clothes) **do you take?**

Quelle pointure faites-vous?
kel pwañtoor feht voo
What size (shoe) **do you take?**

■ **NUMBERS** ■ **PAYING** ■ **SHOPPING**

COTTON	LE COTON	SILK	LA SOIE
LACE	LA DENTELLE	SUEDE	LE DAIM
LEATHER	LE CUIR	WOOL	LA LAINE

belt	la ceinture	sañtoor
blouse	le chemisier	shuhmee-zzay
bra	le soutien-gorge	soo-tyañ gorzh
coat	le manteau	moñtoh
dress	la robe	rob
dressing gown	le peignoir	peh-nywar
gloves	les gants	goñ
hat	le chapeau	shapoh
jacket	la veste	vest
knickers	le slip	sleep
nightdress	la chemise de nuit	shuhmeez duh nwee
pumps	les escarpins	eskarpañ
pyjamas	le pyjama	pee-zhama
raincoat	l'imperméable	añ-pehrmay-abl
sandals	les sandales	soñdal
scarf (silk)	le foulard	foolar
scarf (wool)	l'écharpe	aysharp
shirt	la chemise	shuhmeez
shorts	le short	short
skirt	la jupe	zhoop
slippers	les pantoufles	poñ-toofluh
socks	les chaussettes	shoh-set
suit (woman's)	le tailleur	tye-yur
suit (man's)	le costume	kostoom
swimsuit	le maillot de bain	mye-yoh duh bañ
tights	les collants	koloñ
t-shirt	le t-shirt	tee-shurt
tracksuit	le survêtement	soorvet-moñ
trousers	le pantalon	poñta-loñ
zip	la fermeture éclair	fehrm-toor ayklehr

Two key words for describing colours in French are:
clair   light   **foncé**   dark

black	**noir**	*nwar*
blue	**bleu**	*bluh*
navy blue	**bleu marine**	*bluh mareen*
turquoise	**bleu turquoise**	*bluh toorkwaz*
brown	**marron**	*maroñ*
crimson	**pourpre**	*poorpr*
gold	**couleur or**	*koolur or*
green	**vert**	*vehr*
grey	**gris**	*gree*
orange	**orange**	*oroñzh*
pink	**rose**	*roz*
shocking pink	**rose vif**	*roz veef*
purple	**violet**	*vee-olay*
red	**rouge**	*roozh*
bright red	**vermeil**	*vermay*
silver	**couleur argent**	*koolur ar-zhoñ*
white	**blanc**	*bloñ*
yellow	**jaune**	*zhohn*

■ SHAPE

big	**grand(e)**	*groñ(d)*
fat	**gros(se)**	*groh(s)*
flat	**plat(e)**	*pla(t)*
long	**long(ue)**	*loñ(g)*
narrow	**étroit(e)**	*ay-trwa(t)*
round	**rond(e)**	*roñ(d)*
small	**petit(e)**	*puhtee(t)*
square	**carré(e)**	*karay*
tall	**grand(e)**	*groñ(d)*
thick	**épais(se)**	*aypeh(s)*
thin	**mince**	*mañs*
tiny	**tout petit(e)**	*too puhtee(t)*
wide	**large**	*larzh*

This doesn't work
Ça ne marche pas
sa nuh marsh pa

The ... doesn't work
Le/La ... ne marche pas
luh/la ... nuh marsh pa

The ... don't work
Les ... ne marchent pas
lay ... nuh marsh pa

light	**lock**	**heating**	**air conditioning**
la lumière	la serrure	le chauffage	la climatisation
la loo-myehr	*la sehroor*	*luh shohfazh*	*la kleema-teeza-syoñ*

There's a problem with the room...
Il y a un (petit) problème avec la chambre...
eel ya uñ (puhtee) problem avek la shoñbr...

It's noisy
Elle est bruyante
el eh broo-yoñt

It's too hot...
Il fait trop chaud...
eel feh troh shoh...

It's too cold...
Il fait trop froid...
eel feh troh frwa...

in my room
dans ma chambre
doñ ma shoñbr

It's too hot / too cold (food)
C'est trop chaud / trop froid
say troh shoh / troh frwa

The meat is cold
La viande est froide
la vyoñd eh frwad

This isn't what I ordered
Ce n'est pas ce que j'ai commandé
suh neh pa suh kuh zhay komoñday

To whom should I complain?
À qui dois-je m'adresser pour faire une réclamation?
a kee dwa-zh madressay poor fehr oon rayklama-syoñ

It's faulty
Il y a un défaut
eel ya uñ dayfoh

I want a refund
Je veux être remboursé(e)
zhuh vuh etr roñboor-say

The goods were damaged in transit
Les marchandises ont été endommagées pendant le transport
lay marshoñdeez oñ aytay oñdomazhay poñdoñ luh troñspor

■ PROBLEMS ■ REPAIRS ■ ROOM SERVICE

COMPUTER	L'ORDINATEUR
DTP	**PAO** (publication assistée par ordinateur)
FILE	LE FICHIER
FLOPPY DISK	LA DISQUETTE
FONT	LA POLICE
HARD DISK	LE DISQUE DUR
PRINT-OUT	LE LISTING
DATABASE	LA BASE DE DONNÉES
MENU	LE MENU
SOFTWARE PACKAGE	LE PROGICIEL

What computer do you use?
Qu'est-ce que vous utilisez comme ordinateur?
kes kuh vooz ooteelee-zay kom ordeena-tur

Is it IBM compatible?
Est-ce qu'il est compatible avec l'IBM?
es keel eh koñpateebluh avek lee-bay-em

Do you have E-mail?
Avez-vous le courrier électronique?
avay voo luh koor-yay aylek-tro-neek

What is your address?
Quelle est votre adresse?
kel eh votr adress

Do you have a database?
Avez-vous une base de données?
avay voo oon baz duh donay

Do you update it regularly?
Vous la mettez à jour souvent?
voo la metay a zhoor soovoñ

Can you send it on a floppy disk?
Pouvez-vous l'envoyer sur une disquette?
poovay voo loñvwa-yay soor oon dees-ket

What word processing package do you use?
Quelle sorte de traitement de texte utilisez-vous?
kel sort duh treht-moñ duh text ooteelee-zay voo

■ **OFFICE**

With the single European Market, EC citizens are subject only to highly selective spot checks and they can go through the blue customs channel (unless they have goods to declare). There will be no restriction, either by quantity or value, on goods purchased by EC travellers in another EC country provided that they are **for their own personal use**. If you are unsure of certain items, check with the customs officials as to whether duty is required.

CONTRÔLE DES PASSEPORTS	PASSPORT CONTROL
CE	EC
AUTRES PASSEPORTS	OTHER PASSPORTS
MAGASIN HORS-TAXE	DUTY-FREE SHOP
DOUANE	CUSTOMS

Do I have to pay duty on this?
Est-ce que je dois payer des droits de douane sur ça?
es kuh zhuh dwa pay-yay day drwa duh dwan soor sa

I bought this as a gift
Je l'ai acheté comme cadeau
zhuh lay ashtay kom kadoh

It is for my own personal use
C'est pour mon usage personnel
say poor moñ oo-zazh pehr-sonel

We are on our way to... (if in transit through a country)
Nous allons en...
nooz aloñ oñ...

The children are on this passport
Les enfants sont sur ce passeport
layz oñfoñ soñ soor suh paspor

DAYS, MONTHS & SEASONS — ENGLISH-FRENCH

days

MONDAY	LUNDI
TUESDAY	MARDI
WEDNESDAY	MERCREDI
THURSDAY	JEUDI
FRIDAY	VENDREDI
SATURDAY	SAMEDI
SUNDAY	DIMANCHE

seasons

SPRING	LE PRINTEMPS
SUMMER	L'ÉTÉ
AUTUMN	L'AUTOMNE
WINTER	L'HIVER

months

JANUARY	JANVIER
FEBRUARY	FÉVRIER
MARCH	MARS
APRIL	AVRIL
MAY	MAI
JUNE	JUIN
JULY	JUILLET
AUGUST	AOÛT
SEPTEMBER	SEPTEMBRE
OCTOBER	OCTOBRE
NOVEMBER	NOVEMBRE
DECEMBER	DÉCEMBRE

What is today's date?
Quelle est la date aujourd'hui?
kel eh la dat oh-zhoor-dwee

What day is it today?
Quel jour sommes-nous aujourd'hui?
kel zhoor som noo oh-zhoor-dwee

It's the 5th of March
Nous sommes le 5 mars
noo som luh sañk mars

1st January
le premier janvier
luh pruhm-yay zhoñvee-ay

on Saturday
samedi
samdee

on Saturdays
le samedi
luh samdee

every Saturday
tous les samedis
too lay samdee

this Saturday
samedi qui vient
samdee kee vyañ

next Saturday
samedi prochain
samdee proshañ

last Saturday
samedi dernier
samdee dehr-nyay

in June
en juin
oñ zhwañ

at the beginning of June
début juin
dayboo zhwañ

at the end of June
à la fin juin
a la fañ zhwañ

before summer
avant l'été
avoñ laytay

during the summer
pendant l'été
poñdoñ laytay

after summer
après l'été
apreh laytay

■ NUMBERS

ENGLISH·FRENCH — DENTIST

FILLING	UN PLOMBAGE
CROWN	UNE COURONNE
DENTURES	LE DENTIER
A TEMPORARY REPAIR	UN PANSEMENT TEMPORAIRE

I need to see a dentist
J'ai besoin de voir un dentiste
zhay buhzwañ duh vwar uñ doñteest

He / She has toothache
Il / Elle a mal aux dents
eel / el a mal oh doñ

Can you do a temporary filling?
Pouvez-vous me faire un plombage momentané?
poovay voo muh fehr uñ ploñbazh momoñtanay

It hurts
Ça me fait mal
sa muh feh mal

Can you give me something for the pain?
Pouvez-vous me donner quelque chose
contre la douleur? *poovay voo muh donay
kelkuh shohz koñtr la doo-lur*

I think I have an abscess
Je crois que j'ai un abcès
zhuh crwa kuh zhay uñ abseh

Can you repair my dentures?
Pouvez-vous me réparer mon dentier?
poovay voo muh raypa-ray moñ doñtay

Do I have to pay?
Je dois payer?
zhuh dwa payay

How much will it be?
Combien ça va coûter?
koñ-byañ sa va kootay

I need a receipt for my insurance
Il me faut un reçu pour mon assurance
eel muh foh uñ ruhsoo poor moñ asoo-roñs

■ YOU MAY HEAR

Il faut l'arracher
eel foh larashay
It has to come out

Je vais vous faire une piqûre
zhuh vay voo fehr oon peekoor
I'm going to give you an injection

OPPOSITE	EN FACE DE	*oñ fas duh*
NEXT TO	À CÔTÉ DE	*a kotay duh*
NEAR TO	PRÈS DE	*preh duh*
TRAFFIC LIGHTS	LES FEUX	*lay fuh*
CROSSROAD	LE CARREFOUR	*luh karfoor*
AT THE CORNER (of road)	AU COIN (de la rue)	*oh kwañ (duh la roo)*

Excuse me, sir / madam!
Pardon, monsieur / madame!
pardoñ muhsyuh / madam

How do I get to...?
Pour aller à/au (etc.)...?
poor alay a/oh ...

to the station
à la gare
a la gar

to the Louvre
au Louvre
oh loovr

Is it far?
C'est loin?
say lwañ

We're looking for...
Nous cherchons...
noo shehrshoñ...

Can we walk there?
Est-ce qu'on peut y aller à pied?
es koñ puh ee alay a pyay

We're lost
Nous nous sommes perdus
noo noo som perdoo

Is this the right way to...?
C'est la bonne direction pour...?
say la bon deerek-syoñ poor...

How do I/we get onto the motorway?
Pour rejoindre l'autoroute, s'il vous plaît?
poor ruhzhwañdr lohto-root seel voo pleh

Can you show me on the map?
Pouvez-vous me montrer sur la carte?
poovay voo me moñtray soor la kart

■ **YOU MAY HEAR**

Tournez à gauche / à droite
toornay a gohsh / a drwat
Turn left / right

Continuez tout droit
konteenoo-ay too drwa
Keep straight on

C'est indiqué
say añdee-kay
It's signposted

C'est au coin de la rue
say oh kwañ duh la roo
It's on the corner of the street

■ BASICS ■ MAPS, GUIDES & NEWSPAPERS

What facilities do you have for disabled people?
Qu'est-ce que vous avez comme aménagements pour les handicapés? *kes kuh vooz avay kom amay-nazh-moñ poor layz oñdeekapay*

Are there any toilets for the disabled?
Est-ce qu'il y a des toilettes pour handicapés? *es keel ya day twalet poor oñdeekapay*

Do you have any bedrooms on the ground floor?
Avez-vous des chambres au rez-de-chaussée? *avay voo day shoñbr oh ray duh shohsay*

Is there a lift?
Est-ce qu'il y a un ascenseur? *es keel ya uñ asoñ-sur*

Where is the lift?
Où est l'ascenseur? *oo eh lasoñ-sur*

Are there any ramps?
Est-ce qu'il y a des rampes? *es keel ya day roñp*

How many steps are there?
Il y a combien de marches? *eel ya koñ-byañ duh marsh*

How wide is the entrance door?
Quelle est la largeur de la porte d'entrée? *kel eh la lar-zhur duh la port doñtray*

Where is the wheelchair accessible entrance?
Où est l'entrée pour les fauteuils roulants? *oo eh loñtray poor lay foht-uhy rooloñ*

Is there a reduction for handicapped people?
Est-ce qu'il y a un rabais pour les handicapés? *es keel ya uñ rabeh poor layz oñdeekapay*

Is there somewhere I can sit down?
Est-ce qu'il y a un endroit où on peut s'asseoir? *es keel ya uñ oñ-drwa oo oñ puh saswar*

■ **ACCOMMODATION** ■ **HOTEL**

DOCTOR ──────────────────── ENGLISH-FRENCH

HÔPITAL	**HOSPITAL**
SERVICE DES URGENCES	**CASUALTY DEPARTMENT**
HORAIRE DES CONSULTATIONS	**SURGERY HOURS**

I need a doctor
J'ai besoin d'un médecin
zhay buh-zwañ duñ maydsañ

I have a pain here (point)
J'ai mal ici
zhay mal eesee

My son / My daughter is ill
Mon fils / Ma fille est malade
moñ fees / ma feey eh malad

He / She has a temperature
Il / Elle a de la fièvre
eel / el a duh la fyeh-vr

I'm diabetic
Je suis diabétique
zhuh swee dya-bay-teek

I'm pregnant
Je suis enceinte
zhuh swee oñsañt

I'm on the pill
Je prends la pilule
zhuh proñ la peelool

I'm allergic to penicillin
Je suis allergique à la penicilline
zhuh swee alehr-zheek a la paynee-seeleen

My blood group is...
Mon groupe sanguin est...
moñ groop soñgañ eh...

Will he have to go to hospital?
Faut-il le transporter à l'hôpital?
foh-teel luh troñsportay a lopee-tal

Will I have to pay?
Est-ce que je dois payer?
es kuh zhuh dwa pay-yay

How much will it cost?
Combien ça va coûter?
koñ-byañ sa va kootay

I need a receipt for the insurance
Il me faut un reçu pour l'assurance
eel muh foh uñ ruhsoo poor lasoo-roñs

■ **YOU MAY HEAR**

Il faut vous transporter à l'hôpital
eel foh voo troñsportay a lopee-tal
You will have to go to hospital

Ce n'est pas très grave
suh neh pa treh grav
It's not serious

■ **BODY** ■ **EMERGENCIES** ■ **PHARMACY**

36

> If you just ask for **un café** you will be served a small strong black coffee. You should specify the type of coffee you want:
>
> | | | |
> |---|---|---|
> | UN CAFÉ CRÈME | uñ kafay krem | WHITE COFFEE |
> | UN GRAND CRÈME | uñ groñ krem | LARGE WHITE COFFEE |
> | UN CAFÉ AU LAIT | uñ kafay oh leh | COFFEE WITH HOT MILK |

a coffee	a sweet cider	an orangeade	...please
un café	un cidre doux	une orangeade	...s'il vous plaît
uñ kafay	uñ seedr doo	oon oroñzhad	...seel voo pleh

a tea...	with milk	with lemon	no sugar
un thé...	au lait	au citron	sans sucre
uñ tay...	oh leh	oh seetroñ	soñ sookr

for two	for me	for him / her	for us
pour deux personnes	pour moi	pour lui / elle	pour nous
poor duh pehr-son	poor mwa	poor lwee / el	poor noo

with ice, please
avec des glaçons, s'il vous plaît
avek day glasoñ seel voo pleh

Some mineral water	sparkling / still
De l'eau minérale	gazeuse / plate (non-gazeuse)
duh loh meenay-ral	gazuhz / plat (noñ gazuhz)

Would you like to have a drink?	What will you have?
Vous voulez prendre quelque chose?	Qu'est-ce que vous prenez?
voo voolay proñdr kelkuh shohz	kes kuh voo pruhnay

I'm very thirsty	It's my round!	I'm paying!
J'ai très soif	C'est ma tournée!	C'est moi qui paie!
zhay treh swaf	say ma toornay	say mwa kee pay

■ **OTHER DRINKS TO TRY**

un chocolat rich-tasting hot chocolate
un citron pressé freshly-squeezed lemon: add water and sugar
un diabolo mint cordial and lemonade
une tisane herb tea: **verveine** verbena, **tilleul** lime

■ **EATING OUT** ■ **WINES & SPIRITS**

For those who are vegetarian, or who prefer vegetarian dishes, turn to the VEGETARIAN topic for further phrases.

Where can we have a snack?
Où est-ce qu'on peut manger un casse-croûte?
oo es koñ puh moñ-zhay uñ kass kroot

Can you recommend a good local restaurant?
Pouvez-vous nous recommander un bon restaurant dans la région?
poovay voo noo ruhko-moñday uñ boñ resto-roñ doñ la ray-zhyoñ

I'd like to book a table for ... people
Je voudrais réserver une table pour ... personnes
zhuh voodray rayzehr-vay oon tabl poor ... pehr-son

for tonight
pour ce soir
poor suh swar

for tomorrow night
pour demain soir
poor duhmañ swar

at 7.30
à dix-neuf heures trente
a deez-nuhf ur troñt

The menu, please
Le menu, s'il vous plaît
luh muhnoo seel voo pleh

What is the dish of the day?
Quel est le plat du jour?
kel eh luh pla doo zhoor

Have you...?
Avez-vous...?
avay voo...

a tourist menu
un menu touristique
uñ muhnoo toorees-teek

a set price menu
un menu à prix fixe
uñ muhnoo a pree feex

Can you recommend a local dish?
Pouvez-vous nous recommander un plat régional?
poovay voo noo ruhko-moñday uñ pla rayzho-nal

What is in this?
Qu'est-ce qu'il y a dedans?
kes keel ya duh doñ

I'll have this
Je prends ça
zhuh proñ sa

More bread...
Encore du pain...
oñkor doo pañ

More water...
Encore de l'eau...
oñkor duh loh

please
s'il vous plaît
seel voo pleh

The bill, please
L'addition, s'il vous plaît
ladee-syoñ seel voo pleh

Is service included?
Est-ce que le service est compris?
es kuh luh sehrvees eh koñpree

38

■ EATING PLACES

Bar *serves drinks, coffee, light breakfasts and often snacks*

Brasserie *cross between a café and restaurant, offering snacks and a limited range of dishes throughout the day*

Crêperie *pancake house offering sweet and savoury pancakes*

Relais routier *roadside restaurant for lorry drivers and also the hungry tourist who wants value for money. They serve set meals, often with drink included –* **boisson comprise**

■ THE MENU

ENTRÉES / HORS D'ŒUVRES	**STARTER**
potage	**soup**
assiete anglaise	**selection of cold meat**
PLAT DE RÉSISTANCE	**MAIN COURSE**
viandes	**meat dishes**
gibier et volaille	**game and poultry**
poissons	**fish**

■ TYPES OF MEAT & POULTRY

agneau *lamb*
bifteck *steak*
bœuf *beef*
blanquette de veau *stewed veal in white wine*
bouchées à la reine *chicken vol au vents*
boudin blanc / noir *white / black pudding*
boulettes *meatballs*
brochette *kebab*
cabri *kid*
caille *quail*
canard *duck*
cervelas *saveloy*
cervelle *brains*
chateaubriand *fillet steak*
chevreuil *venison*

CONT...

coq au vin *chicken cooked in wine*
côte / côtelette *chop, cutlet*
cuisses de grenouille *frogs' legs*
dinde *turkey*
entrecôte *rib steak*
escalope de veau *veal escalope*
escargots *snails*
faisan *pheasant*
filet (mignon) *fillet (small)*
foie *liver:* **foie gras** *goose liver pâté*
gigot d'agneau *leg of lamb*
jambon *ham:* **cru** *cured,* **cuit** *cooked*
lapin *rabbit*
lièvre *hare*
mouton *mutton*
oie *goose*
perdrix *partridge*
porc *pork*
pot-au-feu *beef stew*
poulet *chicken*
poussin *young chicken*
ris de veau *calf's sweetbreads*
rognons *kidney*
rosbif *roastbeef*
sanglier *wild boar*
saucisse / saucisson *sausage / salami*
steack *steak*
tournedos *thick fillet steak*
tripes *tripe*
veau *veal*
volaille *poultry*

■ TYPES OF FISH AND SEAFOOD

anguille	*eel*	huîtres	*oysters*
bisque	*seafood soup*	langouste	*crayfish*
bouillabaisse	*fish soup*	langoustines	*scampi*
cabillaud	*cod*	lotte	*monkfish*
calmar	*squid*	moules	*mussels*
coquilles Saint-Jacques	*scallops*	saumon	*salmon*
fruits de mer	*seafood*	thon	*tuna*
homard	*lobster*	truite	*trout*

■ SALADES ET LÉGUMES   SALAD AND VEGETABLES

chou-fleur	*cauliflower*
petits pois	*peas*
poireau	*leek*
pommes dauphine	*potato croquettes*
pommes frites	*chips*
salade (verte)	*salad (green)*: **salade mixte** *mixed*

■ FROMAGES   CHEESE *(often served before dessert)*

What cheeses do you have?
Qu'est-ce que vous avez comme fromages?
kes kuh vooz avay kom fromazh

un fromage de chèvre	*goat's cheese*
un fromage doux	*a mild cheese*
un fromage du pays	*a local cheese*

■ DESSERTS   DESSERTS

What desserts do you have?
Qu'est-ce que vous avez comme desserts?
kes kuh vooz avay kom dessehr

glace	*ice cream*
mousse au chocolat	*chocolate mousse*
salade de fruits	*fruit salad*

■ DRINKING ■ VEGETARIAN ■ WINES & SPIRITS

POLICE	POLICE
AMBULANCE	AMBULANCE
POMPIERS	FIRE BRIGADE
COMMISSARIAT	POLICE STATION
GENDARMERIE	POLICE STATION (in villages)
LE SERVICE DES URGENCES	CASUALTY DEPARTMENT

Help!
Au secours!
oh skoor

Fire!
Au feu!
oh fuh

Can you help me?
Pouvez-vous m'aider?
poovay voo mayday

There's been an accident!
Il y a eu un accident!
eel ya oo uñ aksee-doñ

Someone has been injured
Il y a un blessé
eel ya uñ blessay

He's been knocked down by a car
Il a été renversé par une voiture
eel a aytay roñvehrsay par oon vwatoor

Please call...
S'il vous plaît, appelez...
seel voo pleh apuhlay...

the police
la police
la polees

an ambulance
une ambulance
oon oñboo-loñs

Where is the police station?
Où est le commissariat?
oo eh luh komee-saree-a

I want to report a theft
je veux signaler un vol
zhuh vuh seen-yalay uñ vol

I've been robbed / attacked
On m'a volé / attaqué
oñ ma volay / ata-kay

Someone's stolen...
On m'a volé...
oñ ma volay...

my bag
mon sac à main
moñ sak a mañ

traveller's cheques
mes travellers
may travellers

My car has been broken into
On a forcé ma voiture
oñ a forsay ma vwatoor

My car has been stolen
On m'a volé ma voiture
oñ ma volay ma vwatoor

I've been raped
On m'a violée
oñ ma vee-o-lay

I want to speak to a policewoman
Je veux parler à une femme gendarme
zhuh vuh parlay a oon fam zhoñdarm

I need to make a telephone call
Il faut que je donne un coup de téléphone
eel foh kuh zhuh don uñ koo duh taylay-fon

I need a report for my insurance
Il me faut un constat pour mon assurance
eel muh foh uñ konsta poor moñ asoo-roñs

I didn't know the speed limit
Je ne connaissais pas la limite de vitesse
zhuh nuh koneh-say pa la leemeet duh vee-tes

How much is the fine?
C'est combien l'amende?
say koñ-byañ lamoñd

Where do I pay it?
Où est-ce que je dois la payer?
oo es kuh zhuh dwa la pay-yay

Do I have to pay it straight away?
Est-ce qu'il faut la payer immédiatement?
es keel foh la pay-yay eemay-dyat-moñ

I'm very sorry, officer
Je suis vraiment désolé(e), monsieur l'agent
zhuh swee vraymoñ dayzo-lay muhsyuh la-zhoñ

■ **YOU MAY HEAR**

Vous avez brûlé un feu rouge
vooz avay broolay uñ fuh roozh
You went through a red light

■ **BODY** ■ **DOCTOR**

43

Check at the local tourist office for information about local events.

What is there to do in the evenings?
Qu'est-ce qu'on peut faire le soir?
kes koñ puh fehr luh swar

Do you have a list of events for this month?
Est-ce que vous avez une liste des festivités pour ce mois-ci?
es kuh vooz avay oon leest day festeeveetay poor suh mwa-see

Is there anything for children?
Est-ce qu'il y a des choses à faire pour les enfants?
es keel ya day shohz a fehr poor layz oñfoñ

Where can I/we get tickets...?
Où est-ce qu'on peut acheter des billets...?
oo es koñ puh ashtay day bee-yay...

for tonight
pour ce soir
poor suh swar

for the show
pour le spectacle
poor luh spek-takl

for the football match
pour le match de football
poor luh match duh foot-bal

I'd like ... tickets
Je voudrais ... billets
zhuh voodray ... bee-yay

...adults
...adultes
...adoolt

...children
...enfants
...oñfoñ

Where can I/we go dancing?
Où est-ce qu'on peut aller danser?
oo es koñ puh alay doñsay

How much is it to get in?
Ça coûte combien l'entrée?
sa koot koñ-byañ loñtray

What time does it open?
À quelle heure est-ce que ça ouvre?
a kel ur es kuh sa oovr

Are there any good shows?
Il y a de bons spectacles?
eel ya duh boñ spek-takl

What do you do at weekends?
Qu'est-ce que vous faites le weekend?
kes kuh voo feht luh weekend

■ CINEMA ■ SIGHTSEEING & TOURIST OFFICE ■ THEATRE

*International codes: France **00 33** (**1**-Paris), Belgium **00 32**,
Luxembourg **00 352**, Switzerland **00 41**.*

ADDRESSING A FAX		
TO	À	
FROM	DE	
DATE	DATE	
RE:	OBJET :	
NUMBER OF PAGES		NOMBRE DE PAGES
PLEASE FIND ATTACHED...		VEUILLEZ TROUVER CI-JOINT...

Do you have a fax?
Avez-vous un fax?
avay voo uñ fax

I want to send a fax
Je voudrais envoyer un fax
zhuh voodray oñvwa-yay uñ fax

What is your fax number?
Quel est votre numéro de fax?
kel eh votr noomayro duh fax

I am having trouble getting through to your fax
J'ai du mal à passer le fax
zhay doo mal a pasay luh fax

Please resend your fax
Veuillez nous renvoyer votre fax
vuh-yay noo roñvwa-yay votr fax

I can't read it
Je ne peux pas le lire
zhuh nuh puh pa luh leer

The fax is constantly engaged
Le fax est constamment occupé
luh fax eh koñstamoñ okoopay

Can I send a fax from here?
Est-ce que je peux envoyer un fax d'ici?
es kuh zhuh puh oñvwa-yay uñ fax deesee

■ LETTERS ■ TELEPHONE

bread	le pain	paň
bread stick	la baguette	ba-get
bread (brown)	le pain complet	paň koňpleh
butter	le beurre	buhr
cereal	les céréales	sayray-al
cheese	le fromage	fromazh
chicken	le poulet	pooleh
coffee (instant)	le café (instantané)	kafay (aňstoň-ta-nay)
cream	la crème	krem
crisps	les chips	sheeps
eggs	les œufs	uh
fish	le poisson	pwasoň
flour	la farine	fareen
ham (cooked)	le jambon cuit	zhoňboň kwee
ham (cured)	le jambon cru	zhoňboň kru
herbal tea	la tisane	tee-zan
honey	le miel	myel
jam	la confiture	koňfee-toor
margarine	la margarine	marga-reen
marmalade	la confiture d'orange	koňfeetoor do-roňzh
milk	le lait	leh
mustard	la moutarde	mootard
oil	l'huile	weel
orange juice	le jus d'orange	zhoo do-roňzh
pasta	les pâtes	pat
pepper	le poivre	pwavr
rice	le riz	ree
salt	le sel	sel
sugar	le sucre	sookr
stock cube	le bouillon cube	boo-yoň koob
tea	le thé	tay
tin of tomatoes	la boîte de tomates	bwat duh tomat
vinegar	le vinaigre	veenaygr
yoghurt	le yaourt	ya-oort

■ FRUIT

apples	les pommes	pom
apricots	les abricots	abreeko
bananas	les bananes	banan
cherries	les cerises	suhreez
grapefruit	le pamplemousse	poñpluh-moos
grapes	le raisin	rezañ
lemon	le citron	seetroñ
melon	le melon	muhloñ
nectarines	les nectarines	nektareen
oranges	les oranges	o-roñzh
peaches	les pêches	pesh
pears	les poires	pwahr
pineapple	l'ananas	ana-na
plums	les prunes	proon
raspberries	les framboises	froñbwaz
strawberries	les fraises	frez

■ VEGETABLES

asparagus	les asperges	asperzh
carrots	les carottes	karot
cauliflower	le chou-fleur	shoo-flur
courgettes	les courgettes	koor-zhet
French beans	les haricots verts	aree-koh vehr
garlic	l'ail	eye
leeks	les poireaux	pwa-roh
lettuce	la laitue	laytoo
mushrooms	les champignons	shoñpee-nyoñ
onions	les oignons	o-nyoñ
peas	les petits pois	puhtee pwa
peppers	les poivrons	pwa-vroñ
potatoes	les pommes de terre	pom duh ter
spinach	les épinards	aypee-nard
tomatoes	les tomates	tomat

*You will find the French quite formal in their greetings, shaking hands both on meeting and parting. **Bonjour, madame** or **bonjour, monsieur** is the politest way to greet someone.*

Hello / Good morning / Good afternoon
Bonjour
boñ-zhoor

Goodbye
Au revoir
oh ruhvwahr

Hi!
Salut!
saloo

Bye!
Salut!
saloo

Good evening
Bonsoir
boñswar

Good night
Bonne nuit
bon nwee

Pleased to meet you
Enchanté(e) de faire votre connaissance
oñshoñ-tay duh fehr votr koneh-soñs

How are you?
Comment allez-vous?
komoñ talay voo

Fine, thanks
Très bien, merci
treh byañ mehrsee

and you?
et vous?
ay voo

See you tomorrow
À demain
a duhmañ

See you soon
À bientôt
a byañtoh

See you later
À tout à l'heure
a too-ta lur

Have a good weekend
Bon weekend
boñ weekend

■ BASICS ■ MAKING FRIENDS

These phrases are intended for use at the hotel desk. More details about rooms can be found in the ACCOMMODATION topic.

Do you have a room for tonight?
Est-ce que vous avez une chambre pour ce soir?
es kuh vooz avay oon shoñbr poor suh swar

I booked a room...
J'ai réservé une chambre...
zhay rayzehr-vay oon shoñbr...

in the name of...
au nom de...
oh noñ duh...

Can I see the room?
Pourrais-je voir la chambre?
pooray zhuh vwar la shoñbr

Have you anything else?
Vous avez autre chose?
vooz avay ohtr shoz

Where can I park the car?
Où est-ce que je peux garer la voiture?
oo es kuh zhuh puh garay la vwatoor

What time is...?
À quelle heure est...?
a kel ur eh...

dinner
le dîner
luh deenay

breakfast
le petit déjeuner
luh puhtee day-zhunay

We'll be back late tonight
Nous rentrerons tard ce soir
noo roñtruh-roñ tar suh swar

Do you lock the door?
Fermez-vous la porte à clé?
fehrmay voo la port a klay

The key, please
La clé, s'il vous plaît
la klay seel voo pleh

Room number...
Chambre numéro...
shoñbr noomayro...

Are there any messages for me?
Il y a des messages pour moi?
eel ya day messazh poor mwa

I'm leaving tomorrow
Je pars demain
zhuh par duhmañ

Please prepare the bill
Pouvez-vous préparer la note
poovay voo praypa-ray la not

Can I leave my luggage until...?
Est-ce que je peux laisser mes bagages jusqu'à...?
es kuh zhuh puh lay-say may bagazh zhoo-ska...

■ ACCOMMODATION ■ ROOM SERVICE

*With the Single European Market, goods within the EC are allowed to travel freely. Businesses supplying goods to VAT-registered EC companies are required to complete a Sales List which accompanies the goods. The VAT (TVA) registration code for France is **FR** followed by the French company's 11-digit number. (Belgium **BE** followed by 8-digit number, Luxembourg **LU** followed by 8-digit number.) VAT is paid at the rate of the destination country.*

What is your VAT registered number?
Quel est votre numéro de TVA?
kel eh votr noomayro duh tay-veh-ah

Our VAT number is... *(GB followed by number)*
Notre numéro de TVA est...
notr noomayro duh tay-veh-ah eh...

The goods should be delivered to...
Les marchandises doivent être livrées à...
lay marshoñdeez dwav etr leevray a...

The consignment must be accompanied by an invoice
L'envoi doit être accompagné d'une facture
loñvwa dwa etr akoñpan-yay doon fak-toor

How long will it take to deliver?
Ça prendra combien de temps à livrer?
sa proñ-dra koñ-byañ duh toñ a leevray

Delivery will take ... days / weeks
La livraison prendra ... jours / semaines
la leevreh-zoñ proñ-dra ... zhoor / smen

Please fax a copy of the pro forma invoice
Veuillez nous faxer une copie de la facture proforma
vuh-yay noo faxay oon kopee duh la fak-toor proforma

Please confirm safe delivery of the goods
Nous vous prions de bien vouloir confirmer la bonne livraison des marchandises *noo voo pree-yoñ duh byañ vool-war koñfeermay la bon leevreh-zoñ day marshoñdeez*

■ NUMBERS ■ OFFICE

PRESSING	DRY-CLEANER'S
LAVERIE AUTOMATIQUE	LAUNDERETTE
LESSIVE EN POUDRE	WASHING POWDER

Where can I do some washing?
Où est-ce que je peux faire un peu de lessive?
oo es kuh zhuh puh fehr uñ puh duh leseev

Do you have a laundry service?
Vous avez un service de blanchisserie?
vooz avay uñ sehrvees duh bloñshees-ree

When will my things be ready?
Mes affaires seront prêtes quand?
mayz afehr suh-roñ pret koñ

Where is...?	the launderette	the dry-cleaner's
Où se trouve...?	la laverie automatique	le pressing
oo suh troov...	*la lav-ree ohto-ma-teek*	*luh pressing*

When does it open?	When does it close?
Ça ouvre à quelle heure?	Ça ferme à quelle heure?
sa oovr a kel ur	*sa fehrm a kel ur*

What coins do I need?
Qu'est-ce qu'il me faut comme pièces de monnaie?
kes keel muh foh kom pyes duh monay

Where can I dry my clothes?
Où est-ce que je peux faire sécher le linge?
oo es kuh zhuh puh fehr sayshay luh lañzh

Can you iron these clothes?
Pouvez-vous repasser ce linge?
poovay voo ruhpa-say suh lañzh

Can I borrow an iron?
Je peux vous emprunter un fer à repasser?
zhuh puh vooz oñprañ-tay uñ fehr a ruhpa-say

■ **ROOM SERVICE**

51

Where can I/we...?
Où est-ce qu'on peut...?
oo es koñ puh...

go fishing
faire de la pêche
fehr duh la pesh

go riding
faire du cheval
fehr doo shuhval

Are there any good beaches near here?
Est-ce qu'il y a de bonnes plages près d'ici?
es keel ya duh boñ plazh preh deesee

sandy
de sable
duh sabluh

Is there a swimming pool?
Est-ce qu'il y a une piscine?
es keel ya oon peeseen

Where can I/we hire mountain bikes?
Où est-ce qu'on peut louer des bicyclettes tout terrain?
oo es koñ puh loo-ay day beesee-klet too teh-rañ

Do you have cycling helmets?
Est-ce que vous avez des casques de cycliste?
es kuh vooz avay day kask duh see-kleest

How much is it...?
C'est combien...?
say koñ-byañ...

per hour
de l'heure
duh lur

per day
par jour
par zhoor

What do you do in your spare time?
Qu'est-ce que vous faites de votre temps libre?
kes kuh voo feht duh votr toñ leebr

I like...
J'aime...
zhem...

to go cycling
faire du vélo
fehr doo vay-lo

sport
faire du sport
fehr doo spor

the theatre
le théâtre
luh tayatr

Are you a member of any clubs?
Est-ce que vous faites partie d'un club?
es kuh voo feht partee duñ club

Do you like playing...?
Vous aimez jouer à/au (etc.)...?
voos ehmay zhoo-ay a/oh...

Do you like...? *(familiar)*
Tu aimes...?
t-ehm...

■ CINEMA ■ MUSIC ■ SPORTS ■ TELEVISION ■ WALKING

Tuesday 17 May 1994	mardi le 17 mai 1994

Dear Sirs	Messieurs *(commercial letter)*
Dear Sir/Madam	Monsieur/Madame
Yours faithfully	Nous vous prions d'agréer, Monsieur/Madame, l'expression de nos salutations distinguées

Dear Mr.../Mrs...	Cher Monsieur.../Chère Madame...
Yours sincerely	Nous vous prions d'agréer, M..../Mme..., l'expression de nos sentiments les plus dévoués

Dear Aude	Chère Aude
Best regards	Salutations *or* Cordialement

Dear Pierre	Cher Pierre
Love	Je t'embrasse *or* Grosses bises

Further to your letter of 7 May...
Suite à votre lettre du 7 mai...

Further to our telephone conversation...
Suite à notre conversation téléphonique...

Please find enclosed...
Veuillez trouver ci-joint...

I look forward to hearing from you
Dans l'attente de vous lire

by return [of] post
par retour du courrier

■ FAX ■ OFFICE

RETRAIT DE BAGAGES	BAGGAGE RECLAIM
CONSIGNE (AUTOMATIQUE)	LEFT LUGGAGE OFFICE (LOCKER)
CHARIOT À BAGAGES	LUGGAGE TROLLEY

My luggage hasn't arrived yet
Mes bagages ne sont pas encore arrivés
may bagazh nuh soñ pa oñkor aree-vay

My suitcase has been damaged on the flight
Ma valise a été abîmée pendant le vol
ma valeez a aytay abee-may poñdoñ luh vol

What has happened to the luggage on the flight from...?
Qu'est-ce qui est arrivé aux bagages du vol en provenance de...?
kes kee eh aree-vay oh bagazh doo vol oñ prohvuh-noñs duh...

Can you help me with my luggage, please?
S'il vous plaît, pouvez-vous m'aider à porter mes bagages?
seel voo pleh poovay voo mayday a portay may bagazh

When does the left luggage office open / close?
Quand est-ce que la consigne ouvre / ferme?
koñd es kuh la koñsee-nyuh oovr / fehrm

I'd like to leave this suitcase...
Je voudrais consigner cette valise...
zhuh voodray koñseen-yay set valeez...

until 4 o'clock
jusqu'à seize heures
zhoo-ska sezh ur

overnight
pour la nuit
poor la nwee

till Saturday
jusqu'à samedi
zhoo-ska samdee

Can I leave my luggage here?
Je peux laisser mes bagages ici?
zhuh puh lay-say may bagazh eesee

I'll collect it at...
Je viendrai les chercher à...
zhuh vyañdray lay shehrshay a...

■ YOU MAY HEAR
Vous pourriez les laisser jusqu'à dix-huit heures
voo pooree-ay lay lay-say zhoo-ska deez-weet ur
You may leave your luggage here until 6 o'clock

■ AIR TRAVEL

In this section we have used the familiar form **tu** *for the questions.*

What's your name?
Quel est ton nom?
kel eh toñ noñ

My name is...
Je m'appelle...
zhuh mapel...

How old are you?
Quel âge as-tu?
kel azh a too

I'm ... years old
J'ai ... ans
zhay ... oñ

Are you French?
Tu es français(e)?
too eh froñseh(z)

I'm English / Scottish / American
Je suis anglais(e) / écossais(e) / américain(e)
zhuh swee oñgleh(-z) / aykoseh(z) / amayreekañ(ken)

Where do you live?
Où est-ce que tu habites?
oo es kuh too abeet

Where do you live? *(plural)*
Où est-ce que vous habitez ?
oo es kuh vooz abeetay

I live in London
J'habite à Londres
zhabeeta loñdruh

We live in Glasgow
Nous habitons à Glasgow
nooz abeetoñ a glasgow

I'm still at school
Je suis toujours à l'école
zhuh swee toozhoor a laykol

I work
Je travaille
zhuh travye

I'm retired
Je suis en retraite
zhuh sweez oñ ruhtret

I'm...
Je suis...
zhuh swee...

single
célibataire
sayleeba-tehr

married
marié(e)
maryay

divorced
divorcé(e)
deevor-say

I have...
J'ai...
zhay...

a boyfriend
un petit ami
uñ puhtee amee

a girlfriend
une petite amie
oon puhteet amee

a partner
un(e) ami(e)
uñ (oon) amee

I have ... children
J'ai ... enfants
zhay ... oñfoñ

I have no children
Je n'ai pas d'enfants
zhnay pa doñfoñ

I'm here on holiday / on business / for the weekend
Je suis ici en vacances / en voyage d'affaires / en weekend
zhuh sweez eesee oñ vakoñs / oñ vwayazh dafehr / oñ weekend

■ **LEISURE/INTERESTS** ■ **SPORTS** ■ **WEATHER** ■ **WORK**

Have you...?
Avez-vous...?
avay vooz ...

a map of the town
un plan de la ville
uñ ploñ duh la veel

a map of the region
une carte de la région
oon kart duh la ray-zhyoñ

Can you show me where ... is on the map?
Pouvez-vous me montrer où est ... sur la carte?
poovay voo muh moñtray oo eh ... soor la kart

Do you have a detailed map of the area?
Est-ce que vous avez une carte détaillée de la région?
es kuh vooz avay oon kart day-ta-yay duh la ray-zhyoñ

Can you draw me a map with directions?
Vous pouvez me faire un dessin avec les directions?
voo poovay muh fehr uñ deh-sañ avek lay deerek-syoñ

Do you have a guide book / leaflet in English?
Est-ce que vous avez un guide / une brochure en anglais?
es kuh vooz avay uñ geed / oon bro-shoor oñ oñgleh

I'd like the English language version (of a cassette guide)
Je voudrais la version anglaise (en cassette)
zhuh voodray la vehr-syoñ oñglehz (oñ ka-set)

Where can I/we buy an English newspaper?
Où est-ce qu'on peut acheter des journaux anglais?
oo es koñ puh ashtay day zhoor-noh oñgleh

Do you have any English newspapers / novels?
Est-ce que vous avez des journaux / des romans anglais?
es kuh vooz avay day zhoor-noh / day romoñ oñgleh

When do the English newspapers arrive?
Quand est-ce que vous recevez les journaux anglais?
koñd es kuh voo ruhsuh-vay lay zhoor-noh oñgleh

Please reserve (name newspaper) **for me**
Pouvez-vous me garder un...
poovay voo muh garday uñ...

■ DIRECTIONS ■ SIGHTSEEING & TOURIST OFFICE

■ LIQUIDS

1/2 litre... *(c.1 pint)*	un demi-litre de...	uñ duhmee leetr duh...
a litre of...	un litre de...	uñ leetr duh...
1/2 bottle of...	demi-bouteille de...	duhmee-bootay duh...
a bottle of...	une bouteille de...	oon bootay duh...
a glass of...	un verre de...	uñ vehr duh...

■ WEIGHTS

100 grams	cent grammes de...	soñ gram duh...
1/2 kilo of...*(c.1 lb)*	un demi-kilo de...	uñ duhmee keelo duh...
a kilo of...	un kilo de...	uñ keelo duh...

■ FOOD

a slice of...	une tranche de...	oon troñsh duh...
a portion of...	une portion de...	oon por-syoñ de...
a dozen...	une douzaine de...	oon doozen duh...
a box of...	une boîte de...	oon bwat duh...
a packet of...	un paquet de...	uñ pakay duh...
a tin of...	une boîte de...	oon bwat duh...
a jar of...	un pot de...	uñ poh duh...

■ MISCELLANEOUS

500 francs of...	500 francs de...	sañk soñ froñ duh...
a third	un tiers	uñ tyehr
a quarter	un quart	uñ kar
ten per cent	dix pour cent	dee poor soñ
more...	encore de...	oñkor duh...
less...	moins de...	mwañ duh...
enough of...	assez de...	assay duh...
double	le double	luh doobl
twice	deux fois	duh fwa
three times	trois fois	trwa fwa

■ FOOD ■ SHOPPING

In Paris ticket options include **un carnet de dix tickets** (a book of
10 tickets) which can be used on metro, bus and RER (suburban
lines) or **un billet de tourisme** which covers 7 days' travel.

ENTRÉE	ENTRANCE
SORTIE	WAY OUT/EXIT
LA LIGNE DE MÉTRO	METRO LINE
PARIS-SÉSAME	**PARIS TRAVEL CARD** (metro and bus travel card: 2, 4 and 7 days)
EN DIRECTION DE...	IN THE DIRECTION OF...

Where is the nearest metro?
Où est la station de métro la plus proche?
oo eh la sta-syoñ duh maytro la ploo prosh

How does the ticket machine work?
Comment est-ce que l'automate marche?
komoñ es kuh lohto-mat marsh

I'm going to...
Je vais à...
zhuh veh a...

Do you have a map of the metro?
Est-ce que vous avez un plan du métro?
es kuh vooz avay uñ ploñ doo maytro

How do I get to...?
Pour aller à/au (etc.)...?
poor alay a/oh...

Do I have to change?
Est-ce qu'il faut changer?
es keel foh shoñ-zhay

Which line is it for...?
C'est quelle ligne pour...?
say kel lee-nyuh poor...

In which direction?
Dans quelle direction?
doñ kel deerek-syoñ

What is the next stop?
Quel est le prochain arrêt?
kel eh luh proshañ areh

Excuse me! This is my stop
Pardon! C'est mon arrêt
pardoñ say moñ areh

I want to get off
Je voudrais descendre ici
zhuh voodray dessoñdr eesee

■ **BUS** ■ **TAXI**

Banks are generally open 0900-1630 Monday to Friday, but as this varies you are best advised to go in the morning.

DISTRIBUTEUR	CASH DISPENSER
INSÉREZ VOTRE CARTE	INSERT YOUR CARD
ATTENDEZ S.V.P.	PLEASE WAIT
COMPOSEZ VOTRE CODE SECRET	ENTER YOUR PERSONAL NUMBER
PUIS VALIDEZ	AND PRESS ENTER
RETRAIT ESPÈCES	CASH WITHDRAWAL
TAPEZ LE MONTANT	PRESS AMOUNT REQUIRED
PRENEZ VOS BILLETS	TAKE YOUR CASH

Where can I change some money?
Où est-ce que je peux changer de l'argent?
oo es kuh zhuh puh shoñ-zhay duh lar-zhoñ

I want to change these traveller's cheques
Je voudrais changer ces travellers
zhuh voodray shoñ-zhay say traveller

When does the bank / the bureau de change open / close?
La banque / Le bureau de change ouvre / ferme quand?
la boñk / luh booroh duh shoñzh oovr / fehrm koñ

Can I pay with pounds / dollars?
Est-ce que je peux payer avec des livres sterling / des dollars?
es kuh zhuh puh pay-yay avek day leevr sterling / day dolar

Can I use my credit card to get francs?
Est-ce que je peux utiliser ma carte de crédit pour avoir des francs?
es kuh zhuh puh ooteelee-zay ma kart duh kraydee poor avwar day froñ

Can I use my card with this cash dispenser?
Je peux utiliser ma carte dans ce distributeur?
zhuh puh ooteelee-zay ma kart doñ suh deestreeboo-tur

Do you have any loose change?
Est-ce que vous avez de la monnaie?
es kuh vooz avay duh la monay

■ PAYING

Are there any good concerts on?
Il y a de bons concerts en ce moment?
eel ya duh boñ koñsehr oñ suh momoñ

Where can I get tickets for the concert?
Où est-ce qu'on peut avoir des billets pour le concert?
oo es koñ puh avwar day bee-yay poor luh koñsehr

Where can we hear some classical music / some jazz?
Où est-ce qu'on peut aller écouter de la musique classique / du jazz?
oo es koñ puh alay aykootay duh la moo-zeek klaseek / doo jaz

What sort of music do you like?
Qu'est-ce que vous aimez comme musique?
kes kuh vooz aymay kom moo-zeek

I like...
J'aime...
zhem...

Which is your favourite group / singer?
Quel est votre groupe / chanteur préféré?
kel eh votr groop / shoñtur prayfay-ray

Can you play any musical instrument?
Est-ce que vous savez jouer d'un instrument de musique?
es kuh voo savay zhoo-ay duñ añstroomoñ duh moo-zeek

I play...	the guitar	piano	clarinet
Je joue...	de la guitare	du piano	de la clarinette
zhuh zhoo...	*duh la gee-tar*	*doo pyano*	*duh la klaree-net*

Have you been to any good concerts?
Vous êtes allés à de bons concerts?
vooz eht a-lay a duh boñ koñsehr

Do you like opera?
Vous aimez l'opéra?
vooz aymay lopayra

Do you like reggae?
Tu aimes le reggae? *(familiar)*
t-aym luh reggae

■ ENTERTAINMENT ■ MAKING FRIENDS

0	zéro	*zayro*		**1st**	**premier(ière)**	*pruh-myay (yehr)*
1	un	*uñ*				
2	deux	*duh*		**2nd**	**deuxième**	*duh-zyem*
3	trois	*trwa*				
4	quatre	*katr*		**3rd**	**troisième**	*trwa-zyem*
5	cinq	*sañk*				
6	six	*sees*		**4th**	**quatrième**	*katree-yem*
7	sept	*set*				
8	huit	*weet*		**5th**	**cinquième**	*sañ-kyem*
9	neuf	*nuhf*				
10	dix	*dees*		**6th**	**sixième**	*see-zyem*
11	onze	*oñz*				
12	douze	*dooz*		**7th**	**septième**	*seh-tyem*
13	treize	*trez*				
14	quatorze	*katorz*		**8th**	**huitième**	*wee-tyem*
15	quinze	*kañz*				
16	seize	*sez*		**9th**	**neuvième**	*nuh-vyem*
17	dix-sept	*dees-set*				
18	dix-huit	*deez-weet*		**10th**	**dixième**	*dee-zyem*
19	dix-neuf	*deez-nuhf*				
20	vingt	*vañ*				
21	vingt et un	*vañt ay uñ*				
22	vingt-deux	*vañ-duh*				
23	vingt-trois	*vañ-trwa*				
24	vingt-quatre	*vañ-katr*				
25	vingt-cinq	*vañ-sañk*				
26	vingt-six	*vañ-sees*				
27	vingt-sept	*vañ-set*				
28	vingt-huit	*vañ-weet*				
29	vingt-neuf	*vañ-nuhf*				
30	trente	*troñt*				
40	quarante	*karoñt*				
50	cinquante	*sañkoñt*				
60	soixante	*swasoñt*				
70	soixante-dix	*swasoñt-dees*				
80	quatre-vingts	*katr-vañ*				
90	quatre-vingt-dix	*katr-vañ-dees*				
91	quatre-vingt-onze	*katr-vañ-oñz*				
100	cent	*soñ*				
110	cent dix	*soñ dees*				
200	deux cents	*duh soñ*				
1,000	mille	*meel*				
1 million	un million	*uñ mee-lyoñ*				

AN APPOINTMENT	UN RENDEZ-VOUS
EXTENSION NUMBER	LE NUMÉRO DE POSTE
SWITCHBOARD	LE STANDARD

I'd like to speak to the office manager
Je voudrais parler au chef de bureau
zhuh voodray par-lay oh shef duh booroh

What is your address?
Quelle est votre adresse?
kel eh votr adress

Which floor?
À quel étage?
a kel ay-tazh

Can you make ... photocopies of this?
Pouvez- vous me photocopier ça en ... exemplaires?
poovay voo muh foto-kopyay sa oñ ... exoñplehr

Do you use a courier service?
Est-ce que vous utilisez un service de messagerie?
es kuh vooz ooteelee-zay uñ sehrvees duh messazh-ree

Can you send this for me?
Pouvez-vous envoyer ça pour moi?
poovay voo oñvwa-yay sa poor mwa

What time does the office open / close?
Le bureau ouvre / ferme à quelle heure?
luh booroh oovr / fehrm a kel ur

How do I get to your office?
Pour aller à votre bureau?
poor alay a votr booroh

■ YOU MAY HEAR

Asseyez-vous, je vous en prie
assay-yay voo zhuh vooz oñ pree
Please take a seat

...sera avec vous dans un instant
...suh-ra avek voo doñz uñ añstoñ
...will be with you in just a moment

■ BUSINESS–MEETING ■ FAX ■ LETTERS

BILL *(restaurant)*	L'ADDITION
BILL *(hotel)*	LA NOTE
INVOICE	LA FACTURE
CASH DESK	LA CAISSE

How much is it?
C'est combien? / Ça fait combien?
say koñ-byañ / sa feh koñ-byañ

How much will it be?
Ça fera combien?
sa fuh-ra koñ-byañ

Can I pay...?
Je peux payer...?
zhuh puh pay-yay...

by credit card
avec ma carte de crédit
avek ma kart duh kraydee

by cheque
par chèque
par shek

Do you take credit cards?
Vous acceptez les cartes de crédit?
vooz aksep-tay lay kart duh kraydee

Is...?
Est-ce que...?
es kuh...

service included
le service est compris
luh sehrvees eh koñpree

tax included
la taxe est comprise
la tax eh koñpreez

Put it on my bill
Mettez-le sur la note
metay luh soor la not

Could you give me a receipt, please?
Pourriez-vous me donner un reçu, s'il vous plaît?
pooree-ay voo muh donay uñ ruhsoo seel voo pleh

Do I pay in advance?
Est-ce qu'il faut payer à l'avance?
es keel foh pay-yay ala-voñs

Where do I pay?
Où est-ce qu'il faut payer?
oo es keel foh pay-yay

I'm sorry
Je suis désolé(e)
zhuh swee dayzo-lay

I've nothing smaller *(no change)*
Je n'ai pas de monnaie
zhuh nay pa duh monay

■ MONEY ■ SHOPPING

SUPER	4 STAR
SANS PLOMB	UNLEADED
GAS-OIL	DIESEL
LA BANDE DE ROULEMENT	TREAD OF TYRE
LA ROUE DE SECOURS	SPARE WHEEL

Fill it up, please
Le plein, s'il vous plaît
luh plañ seel voo pleh

Please check the oil / the water
Pouvez-vous vérifier l'huile / l'eau?
poovay voo vayree-fyay lweel / loh

...francs worth of unleaded petrol
...francs d'essence sans plomb
...froñ daysoñs soñ ploñ

Where is...?
Où se trouve...?
oo suh troov...

the air line
le compresseur
le koñpreh-sur

the water
l'eau
loh

Can you check the tyre pressure?
Pouvez-vous vérifier la pression des pneus?
poovay voo vay-ree-fyay la preh-syoñ day pnuh

Please fill this can with petrol
Pouvez-vous remplir ce bidon d'essence?
poovay voo roñpleer suh bee-doñ dessoñs

Where do I pay?
Où dois-je payer?
oo dwa-zhuh pay-yay

Do you take credit cards?
Vous acceptez les cartes de crédit?
vooz aksep-tay lay kart duh kraydee

Do you have distilled water?
Avez-vous de l'eau distillée?
avay voo duh loh deestee-lay

I don't want to change the tyres
Je ne veux pas changer les pneus
zhuh nuh vuh pa shoñ-zhay lay pnuh

I checked the tread
J'ai bien vérifié la bande de roulement
zhay byañ vayree-fyay la boñd duh roo-luh-moñ

■ **BREAKDOWNS** ■ **CAR**

| PHARMACIE (green cross) | PHARMACY/CHEMIST |
| PHARMACIE DE GARDE | DUTY CHEMIST |

I'm ill
Je suis malade
zhuh swee malad

Can you give me something for...?
Avez-vous quelque chose pour le/la (etc.)...?
avay voo kelk shoz poor luh/la...

a headache	car sickness	flu	diarrhoea
le mal de tête	le mal des transports	la grippe	la diarrhée
luh mal duh tet	luh mal day troñspor	la greep	la dya-ray

I've got a temperature
J'ai de la fièvre
zhay duh la fyevr

Is it safe for children?
C'est sans danger pour les enfants?
say soñ doñzhay poor layz oñfoñ

How much should I give them?
Combien je dois leur en donner?
koñ-byañ zhuh dwa lur oñ donay

■ YOU MAY HEAR

Prenez-en trois fois par jour avant / pendant / après le repas
pruhnayzoñ trwa fwa par zhoor avoñ / poñdoñ / apray luh ruhpa
Take it three times a day before / with / after meals

■ WORDS YOU MAY NEED

antiseptic	un antiseptique	oñtee-septeek
aspirin	de l'aspirine	aspee-reen
condoms	les préservatifs	praysehrva-teef
cotton wool	le coton hydrophile	kotoñ eedro-feel
dental floss	du fil dentaire	feel doñtehr
insect repellent	la crème anti-insecte	krem oñtee-añsekt
lip salve	le baume pour les lèvres	bohm poor lay lehvr
period pains	les règles douloureuses	reh-gluh dooloo-ruhz
plasters	le sparadrap	spara-dra
sore throat	le mal de gorge	mal duh gorzh
tampons	les tampons	toñpoñ
toothpaste	le dentifrice	doñtee-frees

■ BODY ■ DOCTOR

Tapes for video cameras and camcorders can be bought in hi-fi shops – magasin hi-fi

Where can I/we buy video tapes for a camcorder?
Où peut-on acheter des cassettes vidéo pour un caméscope?
oo puh-toñ ashtay day ka-set video poor uñ kamay-skop

A colour film...
Une pellicule en couleur...
oon peleekool oñ koo-lur...

with 24 / 36 exposures
avec 24 / 36 poses
avek vañ-katr / troñt-sees poz

A video tape for this camcorder
Une cassette vidéo pour ce caméscope, s'il vous plaît
oon ka-set video poor suh kamay-skop seel voo pleh

Have you batteries...?
Avez-vous des piles...?
avay voo day peel...

for this camera / this camcorder
pour cet appareil / ce caméscope
poor set apa-ray / suh kamay-skop

Can you develop this film?
Pouvez-vous développer cette pellicule?
poovay voo day-vlopay set peleekool

I'd like mat / glossy prints
Je voudrais des photos mates / brillantes
zhuh voodray day foto mat / bree-yoñt

When will the photos be ready?
Quand est-ce que les photos seront prêtes?
koñd es kuh lay foto suh-roñ pret

The film is stuck
La pellicule est coincée
la peleekool eh kwañ-say

Can you take it out for me?
Pouvez-vous me l'enlever?
poovay voo muh loñ-luhvay

Is it OK to take pictures here?
Est-ce qu'on peut prendre des photos ici?
es koñ puh proñdr day foto eesee

Would you take a picture of us, please?
Est-ce que vous pourriez nous prendre en photo, s'il vous plaît?
es kuh voo pooree-ay noo proñdr oñ foto seel voo pleh

■ SHOPPING

Post Offices are generally shut for lunch (approx.1200-1400).

POST OFFICE	LA POSTE / LES **PTT**
POSTBOX	LA BOÎTE AUX LETTRES
STAMPS	LES TIMBRES

Is there a post office near here?
Il y a un bureau de poste près d'ici?
eel ya uñ booroh duh post preh deesee

When is it open?
C'est ouvert quand?
say oovehr koñ

Which counter...?
C'est quel guichet...?
say kel gee-shay...

for stamps
pour les timbres
poor lay tañbr

for parcels
pour les colis
poor lay kolee

Three stamps for postcards to Great Britain
Trois timbres pour cartes postales pour la Grande Bretagne
trwa tañbr poor kart pos-tal poor la groñd bruhta-nyuh

I want to send this letter registered post
Je voudrais envoyer cette lettre en recommandé
zhuh voodray oñvwa-yay set letr oñ ruhkomoñ-day

How much is it to send this parcel?
C'est combien pour envoyer ce colis?
say koñ-byañ poor oñvwa-yay suh kolee

by air
par avion
par a-vyoñ

by surface mail
par voie normale
par vwa normal

It's a gift
C'est un cadeau
say uñ kadoh

The value of contents is ... francs
La valeur est de... francs
la va-lur eh duh ... froñ

■ YOU MAY HEAR

Vous pouvez acheter les timbres au tabac
voo poovay ashtay lay tañbr oh taba
You can buy stamps at the tobacconist's

■ DIRECTIONS

Can you help me?
Pouvez-vous m'aider?
poovay voo mayday

I speak very little French
Je parle très peu le français
zhuh parl treh puh luh froñseh

Does anyone here speak English?
Est-ce qu'il y a quelqu'un qui parle anglais ici?
es keel ya kelkuñ kee parl oñgleh eesee

What's the matter?
Qu'est-ce qui se passe?
kes kee suh pass

I would like to speak to whoever is in charge
Je voudrais parler avec le responsable
zhuh voodray parlay avek luh ruhspoñ-sabl

I'm lost
Je me suis perdu(e)
zhuh muh swee pehrdoo

How do I get to...?
pour aller à/au (etc.)...?
poor alay a/oh...

I missed...	**my train**	**my plane**	**my connection**
J'ai manqué...	mon train	mon avion	ma correspondance
zhay moñkay...	*moñ trañ*	*moñ a-vyoñ*	*ma kores-poñ-doñs*

I've missed my flight because there was a strike
J'ai manqué mon avion à cause d'une grève
zhay moñkay moñ a-vyoñ a kohz doon grehv

The coach has left without me
Le car est parti sans moi
luh kar eh partee soñ mwa

Can you show me how this works?
Pouvez-vous me montrer comment ça marche?
poovay voo muh moñtray komoñ sa marsh

I have lost my purse
`J'ai perdu mon porte-monnaie
zhay pehrdoo moñ port-monay

I need to get to...
Je dois aller à/au (etc.)...
zhuh dwa alay a/oh...

Leave me alone!
Laissez-moi tranquille!
laysay mwa troñkeel

Go away!
Allez-vous en!
alay vooz oñ

■ **COMPLAINTS** ■ **EMERGENCIES**

Do you have...?
Est-ce que vous avez...?
es kuh vooz avay...

When...?
Quand...?
koñ...

At what time...?
À quelle heure...?
a kel ur...

Where is / are...?
Où est / sont
oo eh / soñ

Where is (are)...?
Où se trouve(nt)...?
oo suh troov...

Can I...?
Est-ce que je peux...?
es kuh zhuh puh...

Can we...?
Est-ce que nous pouvons...?
es kuh noo poovoñ...

Is it...? / Are they...?
C'est...? / Ce sont...?
seh... / suh soñ...

Is / Are there...?
Est-ce qu'il y a...?
es keel ya...

How far is...?
C'est loin...?
say lwañ...

What time is it?
Quelle heure est-il?
kel ur eht eel

Who are you?
Qui êtes-vous?
kee eht voo

Who...?
Qui...?
kee...

What?
Quoi?
qwa

Why...?
Pourquoi...?
poorkwa...

How much / many...?
Combien...?
koñ-byañ...

How much is it?
C'est combien?
seh koñ-byañ

How...?
Comment...?
komoñ...

Which one?
Lequel / Laquelle?
luhkel / lakel

Where are the toilets?
Où sont les toilettes?
oo soñ lay twalet

■ **BASICS**

| LE CORDONNIER | SHOE REPAIR SHOP |
| RÉPARATIONS MINUTE | REPAIRS WHILE YOU WAIT |

This is broken
C'est cassé
say kassay

Where can I get this repaired?
Où est-ce que je peux le faire réparer?
oo es kuh zhuh puh luh fehr raypa-ray

Is it worth repairing?
Est-ce que ça vaut la peine de le faire réparer?
es kuh sa voh la pehn duh luh fehr raypa-ray

Can you repair...?
Pouvez-vous réparer...?
poovay voo raypa-ray...

these shoes
ces chaussures
say shoh-soor

my watch
ma montre
ma moñtr

How much will it be?
Ça reviendra à combien?
sa ruhvyañ-dra a koñ-byañ

Can you do it straight away?
Vous pouvez le faire tout de suite?
voo poovay luh fehr too d-sweet

How long will it take?
Ça prendra combien de temps?
sa proñd-ra koñ-byañ duh toñ

When will it be ready?
Ça sera prêt quand?
sa suh-ra preh koñ

Where can I have my shoes reheeled?
Où est-ce que je peux faire mettre de nouveaux talons à mes chaussures? *oo es kuh zhuh puh fehr metr duh noovoh taloñ a may shoh-soor*

I need...
Il me faut...
eel muh foh...

some glue
de la colle
duh la kol

some Sellotape®
du scotch®
doo scotch

some buttons
des boutons
day bootoñ

Do you have a needle and thread?
Est-ce que vous avez du fil et une aiguille?
es kuh vooz avay doo feel ay oon aygwee

The lights have fused
Les plombs ont sauté
lay ploñ oñ soh-tay

■ BREAKDOWNS

Come in!
  Entrez!
  oñtray

Please come back later
  Pouvez-vous revenir plus tard?
  poovay voo ruhv-neer ploo tar

I'd like breakfast / a sandwich in my room
  Je voudrais le petit déjeuner / un sandwich dans ma chambre
  zhuh voodray luh puhtee dayzhuh-nay / uñ soñdweech doñ ma shoñbr

Please bring…
  Pouvez-vous m'apporter…
  poovay voo maportay…

a glass
  un verre
  uñ vehr

clean towels
  des serviettes propres
  day sehr-vyet propr

toilet paper
  du papier hygiénique
  doo papyay ee-zhay-neek

I'd like an early morning call at … o'clock tomorrow
  Je voudrais qu'on m'appelle tôt demain matin à … heures
  zhuh voodray koñ mapel toh duhmañ matañ a … ur

I'd like an outside line
  Je voudrais appeler à l'extérieur
  zhuh voodray aplay a lekstay-ree-ur

The … doesn't work
  Le/La … ne marche pas
  luh/la … nuh marsh pa

Please can you repair it
  Est-ce que vous pouvez le/la réparer?
  es kuh voo poovay luh/la raypa-ray

I need more coat hangers
  Il me faudrait encore des cintres
  eel muh foh-dreh eñkor day sañtr

Is there a laundry service?
  Vous avez un service de blanchisserie?
  vooz avay uñ sehrvees duh bloñshees-ree

Is there a trouser press?
  Est-ce qu'il y a une presse-pantalon?
  es keel ya oon press-poñta-loñ

■ HOTEL ■ LAUNDRY ■ TELEPHONE

SHOPPING — ENGLISH-FRENCH

| SOLDES | SALE | UN GRAND MAGASIN | DEPARTMENT STORE |
| AU RABAIS | DISCOUNT | LE RAYON ALIMENTATION | FOOD DEPARTMENT |

Where is the main shopping area?
Pour aller aux magasins?
poor alay oh maga-zañ

I'm looking for a present for...	**my mother**	**a child**
Je cherche un cadeau pour...	ma mère	un enfant
zhuh shehrsh uñ kadoh poor...	*ma mehr*	*uñ oñfoñ*

Where can I buy...?	**toys**	**gifts**
Où est-ce qu'on peut acheter...?	des jouets	des cadeaux
oo es koñ puh ashtay...	*day zhoo-ay*	*day kadoh*

Can you recommend any good shops?
Pouvez-vous me conseiller de bons magasins?
poovay voo muh koñsay-yay duh boñ maga-zañ

Where is the ... department?	**perfume**	**jewellery**
Où se trouve le rayon...?	parfumerie	bijouterie
oo suh troov luh rayoñ...	*parfoom-ree*	*beezhoo-tree*

I'd like something similar to this
Je voudrais quelque chose dans ce genre-là
zhuh voodray kelkuh shohz doñ suh zhoñr la

It's too expensive for me	**Have you anything else?**
C'est trop cher pour moi	Vous n'avez rien d'autre?
say troh shehr poor mwa	*voo navay ryañ dohtr*

Is there a market?	**Which day?**
Est-ce qu'il y a un marché?	Quel jour?
es keel ya uñ marshay	*kel zhoor*

■ **YOU MAY HEAR**

Qu'est-ce que vous désirez?
kes kuh voo dayzeeray
What would you like?

■ **CLOTHES** ■ **MEASUREMENTS & QUANTITIES**

72

Opening hours approx. 0900 - 1900, with some smaller shops closing for lunch (1200-1400).

baker's	BOULANGERIE	booloñ-zhuree
bookshop	LIBRAIRIE	leebreh-ree
butcher's	BOUCHERIE	boosh-ree
butcher's (pork)	CHARCUTERIE	sharkoot-ree
cake shop	PÂTISSERIE	patees-ree
cheese shop	FROMAGERIE	fromazh-ree
clothes	VÊTEMENTS	vetmoñ
DIY	BRICOLAGE	breeko-lazh
dry-cleaner's	PRESSING	presseeng
electrical goods	APPAREILS ÉLECTRIQUES	apa-ray aylek-treek
fishmonger's	POISSONNERIE	pwasoñ-ree
furniture	MEUBLES	muhbluh
gifts	CADEAUX	kadoh
greengrocer's	FRUITS ET LÉGUMES	frwee ay laygoom
grocer's	ÉPICERIE	aypees-ree
hairdresser	COIFFEUSE	kwa-fuz
health food shop	DIÉTÉTIQUE	deeyehtehteek
household articles	ENTRETIEN	oñtruhtyañ
hypermarket	HYPERMARCHÉ	eepehr-marshay
ironmonger's	QUINCAILLERIE	kañkye-yuhree
jeweller's	BIJOUTERIE	beezhoo-tree
market	MARCHÉ	marshay
perfume shop	PARFUMERIE	parfoom-ree
pharmacy	PHARMACIE	farmasee
self-service	LIBRE-SERVICE	leebr-sehrvees
shoe shop	CHAUSSURES	shoh-soor
sports shop	ARTICLES DE SPORT	arteekl duh spor
stationer's	PAPETERIE	paptree
sweet shop	CONFISERIE	koñfees-ree
supermarket	SUPERMARCHÉ	soopehr-marshay
tobacconist's	TABAC	taba
toy shop	JOUETS	zhoo-ay

The tourist office is called le syndicat d'initiative. If you are looking for somewhere to stay they will have details of hotels, campsites, etc. Most museums are closed on Tuesdays.

Where is the tourist office?
Où est le syndicat d'initiative?
oo eh luh sañdee-ka deenee-sya-teev

What is there to visit in the area?
Qu'est-ce qu'il y a à voir dans la région?
kes keel ya a vwar doñ la ray-zhyoñ

in two hours
en deux heures
oñ duhz ur

Have you any leaflets?
Avez-vous de la documentation?
avay voo duh la dohkoh-moñta-syoñ

When can we visit the...?
Quand est-ce qu'on peut visiter le/la...?
koñd es koñ puh veezeetay luh/la...

Are there any excursions?
Est-ce qu'il y a des excursions?
es keel ya dayz ekskoor-syoñ

We'd like to go to...
On voudrait aller à...
oñ voodray alay a...

When does it leave?
À quelle heure part-il?
a kel ur par teel

Where does it leave from?
Il part d'où?
eel par doo

How much does it cost to get in?
C'est combien l'entrée?
say koñ-byañ loñtray

Are there any reductions for...?
Est-ce que vous faites des réductions pour...?
es kuh voo feht day raydook-syoñ poor...

children	**students**	**unemployed**	**senior citizens**
les enfants	les étudiants	les chômeurs	les retraités
layz oñfoñ	*layz aytoo-dyoñ*	*lay shoh-mur*	*lay ruhtretay*

■ ENTERTAINMENT ■ MAPS, GUIDES & NEWSPAPERS

ACCÈS AUX TRAINS
TO THE TRAINS

À LOUER
FOR HIRE / TO RENT

APPUYEZ
PRESS

ARRÊT
STOP

ASCENSEUR
LIFT

À VENDRE
FOR SALE

BAIGNADE INTERDITE
NO BATHING

BILLETS
TICKETS

CAISSE
CASH DESK

CASSE-CROÛTE
SNACKS

CHAMBRES
ROOMS TO LET

COMPLET
NO VACANCIES

COMPOSTER VOTRE BILLET
VALIDATE YOUR TICKET

CONSIGNE
LEFT LUGGAGE

DAMES
LADIES

DÉFENSE DE FUMER
NO SMOKING

DÉFENSE DE MARCHER SUR LES PELOUSES
DO NOT WALK ON THE GRASS

DÉGUSTATION DES VINS
WINE TASTING

EAU POTABLE
DRINKING WATER

EN PANNE
OUT OF ORDER

ENTRÉE
ENTRANCE

FERMÉ
CLOSED

FROID
COLD

FUMEURS
SMOKERS

HOMMES
GENTS

LIBRE
FREE, VACANT

LIBRE-SERVICE
SELF-SERVICE

MESSIEURS
GENTS

NON-FUMEURS
NO SMOKING

OCCUPÉ
ENGAGED

OUVERT
OPEN

POUSSEZ
PUSH

PRIÈRE DE...
PLEASE...

PRIVÉ
PRIVATE

RENSEIGNEMENTS
INFORMATION

REZ-DE-CHAUSSÉE
GROUND FLOOR

SOLDES
SALES

SONNEZ
RING

SORTIE
EXIT

SORTIE DE SECOURS
EMERGENCY EXIT

SOUS-SOL
BASEMENT

TIREZ
PULL

SKI PASS	LE FORFAIT
BEGINNER	DÉBUTANT
INTERMEDIATE	INTERMÉDIAIRE
ADVANCED	AVANCÉ

I want to hire skis
Je voudrais louer des skis
zhuh voodray loo-ay day skee

Are the poles included in the price?
Est-ce que les bâtons sont compris dans le prix?
es kuh lay batoñ soñ koñpree doñ luh pree

Can you adjust my bindings, please?
Pourriez-vous régler mes fixations, s'il vous plaît?
pooree-ay voo rayglay may feeksa-syoñ seel voo pleh

How much is a pass for...?   a day   a week
C'est combien le forfait pour...?   une journée   une semaine
say koñ-byañ luh forfay poor...   *oon zhoor-nay*   *oon smen*

Do you have a map of the pistes?
Avez-vous une carte des pistes?
avay voo oon kart day peest

When does the last chair-lift go up?
À quelle heure part la dernière benne?
a kel ur par la dehr-nyehr ben

■ YOU MAY HEAR

Est-ce que vous avez déjà fait du ski?
es kuh vooz avay day-zha feh doo skee
Have you ever skied before?

Quelle longueur de skis voulez-vous?
kel loñg-ur duh skee voolay voo
What length skis do you want?

Quelle pointure faites-vous?
kel pwañ-toor feht voo
What is your shoe size?

| MATCH / GAME | LE MATCH / LE JEU |
| PITCH / COURT | LE TERRAIN / LE COURT |

Where can I/we...?
Où est-ce qu'on peut...?
oo es koñ puh...

play tennis
jouer au tennis
zhoo-ay oh tenees

play golf
jouer au golf
zhoo-ay oh golf

go swimming
faire de la natation
fehr duh la nata-syoñ

go jogging
faire du jogging
fehr doo jogging

How much is it per hour?
C'est combien l'heure?
say koñ-byañ lur

Do you have to be a member?
Est-ce qu'il faut être membre?
es keel foh etr moñbr

Can we hire...?
Est-ce qu'on peut louer...?
es koñ puh loo-ay...

rackets
des raquettes
day ra-ket

golf clubs
des clubs de golf
day club duh golf

We'd like to go to see (name team) **play**
Nous voudrions aller voir jouer l'équipe de...
noo voo-dryoñ alay vwar zhoo-ay lay-keep duh...

Where can I/we get tickets?
Où est-ce qu'on peut avoir des billets?
oo es koñ puh avvar day bee-yay

Which is your favourite football team?
Quelle est votre équipe de football préférée?
kel eh votr ay-keep duh footbal prayfay-ray

What sports do you play?
Qu'est-ce que vous faites comme sports?
kes kuh voo feht kom spor

■ **YOU MAY HEAR**

Le match vous est transmis en direct depuis...
luh match vooz eh troñsmee oñ deerekt duhpwee...
The match is brought live to you from...

■ **LEISURE/INTERESTS** ■ **SKIING** ■ **WALKING**

All these items can be bought à la papeterie

adhesive tape	le scotch®	scotch
biro	le stylo à bille	steelo a bee
book	le livre	leevr
brown paper	le papier d'emballage	papyay doñbalazh
card (greetings)	la carte d'anniversaire	kart danee-vehrsehr
crayons	les pastels	pastel
envelopes	les enveloppes	oñvuh-lop
exercise book	le cahier	ka-yay
felt-tip pen	le crayon-feutre	kray-yoñ fuhtr
file	le dossier / le fichier	dos-yay / feesh-yay
folder	la chemise	shuhmeez
glue	la colle	kol
ink	l'encre	oñkr
ink cartridge	la cartouche	kartoosh
magazine	la revue	ruhvoo
newspaper	le journal	zhoor-nal
note pad	le bloc-notes	blok-not
paints	la boîte de couleurs	bwat duh koo-lur
paper	le papier	papyay
paperback	le livre de poche	leevr duh posh
paperclip	le trombone	troñbon
pen	le stylo	steelo
pencil	le crayon	kray-yon
pencil sharpener	le taille-crayon	tye-kray-yoñ
postcard	la carte postale	kart pos-tal
rubber	la gomme	gom
ruler	la règle	reh-gluh
stapler	une agrafeuse	agra-fuhz
staples	les agrafes	agraf
writing paper	le papier à lettres	papyay a letr

■ OFFICE ■ SHOPPING

ENGLISH·FRENCH —————————————— TAXI

LA STATION DE TAXIS	TAXI RANK

I want a taxi
Je voudrais un taxi
zhuh voodray uñ taxi

Where can I get a taxi?
Où est-ce que je peux prendre un taxi?
oo es kuh zhuh puh proñdr uñ taxi

Please order me a taxi
Pouvez-vous m'appeler un taxi?
poovay voo ma-play uñ taxi

straight away
tout de suite
too d-sweet

for (time)
pour...
poor...

How much is it going to cost to go to...?
Combien ça va coûter pour aller à/au (etc.)...?
koñ-byañ sa va kootay poor alay a/oh...

to the centre
au centre-ville
oh soñtr veel

to the station
à la gare
a la gar

to the airport
à l'aéroport
a la-ayro-por

to this address
à cette adresse
a set adress

How much is it?
C'est combien?
say koñ-byañ

Why is it so much?
Pourquoi c'est si cher?
poor-kwa say see shehr

It's more than on the meter
C'est plus que sur le compteur
say ploo kuh soor luh koñ-tur

Keep the change
Gardez la monnaie
garday la monay

Sorry, I don't have any change
Je suis désolé(e), je n'ai pas de monnaie
zhuh swee dayzo-lay zhuh nay pa d-monay

I'm in a hurry
Je suis pressé(e)
zhuh swee pressay

Is it far?
C'est loin?
say lwañ

Can you go a little faster?
Pourriez-vous aller un peu plus vite?
pooree-ay voo alay uñ puh ploo veet

I have to catch...
Je dois prendre...
zhuh dwa proñdr...

■ BUS ■ METRO

79

*The international code for France is **00 33** plus the French number you require. For Paris add **1** before the number. Otherwise there are no area codes for France. Other international codes are: Belgium – **00 32**, Luxembourg – **00 352**, Switzerland – **00 41**. To phone the UK from France, dial **19 44** plus the UK area code less the first 0, e.g., London (0)**171** or (0)**181**.*

PHONECARD	**UNE TÉLÉCARTE**
TELEPHONE DIRECTORY	**L'ANNUAIRE** (m)
YELLOW PAGES	**LES PAGES JAUNES**
ANSWERING MACHINE	**UN RÉPONDEUR AUTOMATIQUE**
COLLECT CALL	**UN APPEL EN PCV**
FREEPHONE	**NUMÉRO VERT**
TO BE ON THE PHONE	**ÊTRE AU TÉLÉPHONE**
DIAL THE NUMBER	**NUMÉROTER / COMPOSER LE NUMÉRO**
TO PICK UP / HANG UP	**DÉCROCHER / RACCROCHER**

I want to make a phone call
Je voudrais téléphoner (donner un coup de téléphone)
zhuh voodray taylay-fonay (donay uñ koo duh taylay-fon)

What coins do I need?
J'ai besoin de quelles pièces?
zhay buhzwañ duh kel pyes

Can you show me how this phone works?
Pouvez-vous me montrer comment ce téléphone marche?
poovay voo muh moñtray komoñ suh taylay-fon marsh

Where can I buy a phone card?
Où est-ce que je peux acheter une télécarte?
oo es kuh zhuh puh ashtay oon taylay-kart

Monsieur Brun, please
Monsieur Brun, s'il vous plaît
muhsyuh bruñ seel voo pleh

Extension...
le poste...
luh post...

I'd like to speak to...?
Je voudrais parler à...
zhuh voodray parlay a...

This is Jim Brown
C'est de la part de Jim Brown
say duh la par duh jim brown

It's Mr Brooke
C'est M. Brooke à l'appareil
say muhsyuh brooke a lapa-ray

How do I get an outside line?
Comment on fait pour avoir une ligne extérieure?
komoñ oñ feh poor avvar oon leen-yuh ekstay-ree-ur

I'll call back...
Je vous rappellerai...
zhuh voo ra-pluhray...

later
plus tard
ploo tar

tomorrow
demain
duhmañ

We were cut off
Nous avons été coupés
nooz avoñ aytay koopay

I can't get through
Je ne peux pas avoir le numéro
zhuh nuh puh pa avvar luh noomayro

■ **YOU MAY HEAR**

Âllo
alo
Hello

C'est de la part de qui?
say duh la par duh kee
Who's calling?

Un instant, s'il vous plaît...
uñ añstoñ seel voo pleh...
Just a moment...

Je vous le/la passe
zhuh voo luh/la pass
I'm putting you through

C'est occupé
say okoopay
It's engaged

Pouvez-vous rappeler plus tard?
poovay voo ra-play ploo tar
Please try later

Voulez-vous laisser un message?
voolay voo lay-say uñ messazh
Do you want to leave a message?

Vous êtes en communication avec un répondeur automatique
vooz eht oñ komoo-neeka-syoñ avek uñ raypoñ-dur ohtoma-teek
This is an answering machine

Au bip sonore, veuillez laisser votre message
oh beep soñor vuh-yay lay-say votr messazh
Please leave a message after the tone

■ **BUSINESS–MEETING** ■ **FAX** ■ **OFFICE**

REMOTE CONTROL	LA TÉLÉCOMMANDE
SERIES	UN FEUILLETON
SOAP	UN FEUILLETON À L'EAU DE ROSE
VIDEO RECORDER	UN MAGNÉTOSCOPE
NEWS	LES INFORMATIONS
TO SWITCH ON	METTRE EN MARCHE
TO SWITCH OFF	ÉTEINDRE
PROGRAMME	UNE ÉMISSION
CARTOONS	LES DESSINS ANIMÉS

Where is the television?
Où est la télévision?
oo eh la taylay-veezyoñ

How do you switch it on?
Comment est-ce qu'on la met en marche?
komoñ es koñ la meh oñ marsh

What is on television?
Qu'est-ce qu'il y a à la télévision?
kes keel ya a la taylay-veezyoñ

When is the news?
Les informations sont
à quelle heure?
layz añforma-syoñ soñ a kel ur

Do you have any English-speaking channels?
Est-ce qu'il y a des chaînes en anglais?
es keel ya day shen oñ oñglay

When are the children's programmes?
À quelle heure sont les émissions pour les enfants?
a kel ur soñ layz aymee-syoñ poor layz oñfoñ

Do you have any English videos?
Avez-vous des vidéos en anglais?
avay voo day video oñ oñglay

Could you video this programme?
Pourriez-vous enregistrer cette émission sur magnétoscope?
pooree-ay vooz oñruhzhee-stray set aymee-syoñ soor man-yetoskop

PLAY	LA PIÈCE
PERFORMANCE	LA REPRÉSENTATION
IN THE STALLS	À L'ORCHESTRE
IN THE CIRCLE	AU BALCON
IN THE UPPER CIRCLE	AUX DEUXIÈMES GALERIES
SEAT	LE FAUTEUIL
CLOAKROOM	LE VESTIAIRE

What is on at the theatre?
Qu'est-ce qu'on joue au théâtre?
kes koñ zhoo oh tay-atr

How do we get there?
Pour y aller?
poor ee alay

What prices are the tickets?
C'est combien les billets?
say koñ-byañ lay bee-yay

I'd like two tickets...
Je voudrais deux billets...
zhuh voodray duh bee-yay...

for tonight
pour ce soir
poor suh swar

for tomorrow night
pour demain soir
poor duhmañ swar

for 5th August
pour le cinq août
poor luh sañk oo

in the stalls
à l'orchestre
a lorkestr

in the circle
au balcon
oh balkoñ

in the upper circle
aux deuxièmes galeries
oh duh-zyem gal-ree

How long is the interval?
L'entracte dure combien de temps?
loñtract door koñ-byañ duh toñ

Is there a bar?
Il y a un bar?
eel ya uñ bar

When does the performance begin / end?
Quand est-ce que la représentation commence / finit?
koñd es kuh la ruhpray-zoñta-syoñ komoñs / feenee

I enjoyed the play
J'ai bien aimé la pièce
zhay byañ ehmay la pyes

It was very good
C'était une très bonne pièce
saytay oon treh boñ pyes

■ ENTERTAINMENT ■ LEISURE/INTERESTS

> The 24-hour clock is used a lot more in Europe than in Britain.
> After 1200 midday, it continues: **1300**–treize heures,
> **1400**–quatorze heures, **1500**–quinze heures, etc. until
> **2400**–vingt-quatre heures. With the 24-hour clock, the words
> **quart** (quarter) and **demie** (half) aren't used:

13.15 (1.15pm)	*treize heures quinze*
19.30 (7.30pm)	*dix-neuf heures trente*
22.45 (10.45pm)	*vingt-deux heures quarante-cinq*

What time is it?

Il est quelle heure? / Quelle heure est-il?
eel eh kel ur / kel ur eht-eel

It's ...	2 o'clock	3 o'clock	6 o'clock (etc.)
Il est...	deux heures	trois heures	six heures
eel eh...	*duhz ur*	*trwaz ur*	*seez ur*

It's 1 o'clock	It's midday	It's midnight
Il est une heure	Il est midi	Il est minuit
eel eh oon ur	*eel eh meedee*	*eel eh meenwee*

9	**neuf heures**
	nuhf ur
9.10	**neuf heures dix**
	nuhf ur dees
quarter past 9	**neuf heures et quart**
	nuhf ur ay kar
9.20	**neuf heures vingt**
	nuhf ur vañ
9.30	**neuf heures et demie / neuf heures trente**
	nuhf ur ay duhmee / nuhf ur troñt
9.35	**dix heures moins vingt-cinq**
	deez ur mwañ vañ sañk
quarter to 10	**dix heures moins le quart**
	deez ur mwañ luh kar
10 to 10	**dix heures moins dix**
	deez ur mwañ dees

■ NUMBERS

When does it open / close / begin / finish?
Il ouvre / ferme / commence / finit à quelle heure?
eel oovr / fehrm / komoñs / feenee a kel ur

at 3 o'clock	before 3 o'clock	after 3 o'clock
à trois heures	avant trois heures	après trois heures
a trwaz ur	*avoñ trwaz ur*	*apray trwaz ur*

today	tonight	tomorrow	yesterday
aujourd'hui	ce soir	demain	hier
oh-zhoor-dwee	*suh swar*	*duhmañ*	*yehr*

the day before yesterday	the day after tomorrow
avant-hier	après-demain
avoñt yehr	*apray duhmañ*

in the morning	in the afternoon	in the evening
le matin	l'après-midi	le soir
luh matañ	*lapray meedee*	*luh swar*

this morning	this afternoon	this evening/tonight
ce matin	cet après-midi	ce soir
suh matañ	*set apray meedee*	*suh swar*

It's nearly 6 o'clock
Il est presque six heures
eel eh presk seez ur

at half past 7	at about 10 o'clock
à sept heures et demie	vers dix heures
a set ur ay duhmee	*vehr deez ur*

in an hour's time	in half an hour	two hours ago
dans une heure	dans une demi-heure	il y a deux heures
doñs oon ur	*doñs oon duhmee ur*	*eel ya duhz ur*

soon	early	late	later
bientôt	de bonne heure	tard	plus tard
byañtoh	*duh bon ur*	*tar*	*ploo tar*

I'll do it...	as soon as possible	...at the latest
Je le ferai...	aussitôt que possible	...au plus tard
zhuh luh fuh-ray...	*ohsee-toh kuh po-seebl*	*...oh ploo tar*

Before you catch your train, you must validate your ticket in the machines situated on the platforms and which carry the warning **n'oubliez pas de composter votre billet**. *If you fail to do so, you are liable to a fine equal to the amount of the ticket.*

SNCF *(Société nationale des chemins de fer français)*	**FRENCH NATIONAL RAILWAYS**
RER *(Réseau express régional)*	**PARIS REGION HIGH-SPEED SERVICE**
TGV *(train à grande vitesse)*	**HIGH-SPEED INTERCITY** *(reservations compulsory)*
GUICHET	**TICKET OFFICE**
ACCÈS AUX QUAIS	**TO THE PLATFORMS**

When is the next train to....?
Quand part le prochain train pour...?
koñ par luh proshañ trañ poor...

Two return tickets to...
Deux aller et retour pour...
duhz alay ay ruhtoor poor...

A single to...
Un aller simple pour...
uñ alay sañpl poor...

First class / Second class
Première classe / Deuxième classe
pruhm-yehr klas / duh-zyem klas

Smoking / Non smoking
Fumeur / Non fumeur
foo-mur / noñ foo-mur

Is there a supplement to pay?
Y a-t-il un supplément à payer?
ee a-teel uñ sooplay-moñ a pay-yay

I want to book a seat on the TGV to Nîmes
Je voudrais réserver une place dans le TGV pour Nîmes
zhuh voodray rayzehr-vay oon plas doñ luh tay zhay vay poor neem

When is the first / last train to...?
Le premier / Le dernier train pour ... est à quelle heure?
luh pruhm-yay / luh dehr-nyay trañ poor ... eh a kel ur

When does it arrive in...?
À quelle heure arrive-t-il à...?
a kel ur a-reev-teel a...

Do I have to change?
Est-ce qu'il faut changer?
es keel foh shoñ-zhay

How long do I have to catch the connection?
Combien de temps est-ce que j'ai pour prendre la
correspondance? *koñ-byañ duh toñ es kuh zhay poor proñdr la*
kores-poñdoñs

Which platform does it leave from?
Il part de quel quai?
eel par duh kel kay

Is this the right platform for the train to Paris?
Est-ce que c'est le bon quai pour le train de Paris?
es kuh say luh boñ kay poor luh trañ duh paree

Is this the train for...?
C'est le train pour...?
say luh trañ poor...

When will it leave?
Quand est-ce qu'il va partir?
koñd es keel va parteer

Why is the train delayed?
Pourquoi est-ce que le train a du retard?
poor-kwa es kuh luh trañ a doo ruhtar

Does the train stop at...?
Est-ce que le train s'arrête à...?
es kuh luh trañ sareht a...

Where do I change for...?
Où dois-je changer pour...?
oo dwa zhuh shoñ-zhay poor...

Please tell me when we get to...
S'il vous plaît, prévenez-moi, quand nous serons à...
seel voo pleh pray-vnay mwa koñ noo suh-roñs a...

Is there a buffet on the train?
Est-ce qu'il y a un buffet dans le train?
es keel ya uñ boofay doñ luh trañ

Is this seat free?
Cette place est-elle libre?
set plas eh-tel leebr

Excuse me
Excusez-moi
ekskoozay-mwa

Sorry!
Pardon!
pardoñ

■ **LUGGAGE**

Don't expect great things – the French love good meat!

Are there any vegetarian restaurants here?
Est-ce qu'il y a des restaurants végétariens ici?
es keel ya day resto-roň vay-zhayta-ryaň eesee

Do you have any vegetarian dishes?
Vous avez des plats végétariens?
vooz avay day pla vay-zhayta-ryaň

Which dishes have no meat / fish?
Quels sont les plats qui n'ont pas de viande / de poisson?
kel soň lay pla kee noň pa duh vyoňd / duh pwasoň

What fish dishes do you have?
Qu'est-ce que vous avez comme poissons?
kes kuh vooz avay kom pwasoň

I'd like pasta as a main course
Je voudrais des pâtes comme plat de résistance
zhuh voodray day pat kom pla duh rayzee-stoňs

I don't like meat
Je n'aime pas la viande
zhuh nehm pa la vyoňd

What do you recommend?
Qu'est-ce que vous me conseillez?
kes kuh voo muh koňsay-yay

Is it made with vegetable stock?
Est-ce que c'est fait avec du bouillon de légumes?
es kuh say feh avek doo boo-yoň duh laygoom

■ POSSIBLE DISHES

tagliatelles *pasta*
salade verte *green salad:* **niçoise** *tomatoes, olives, tuna, eggs*
artichauts à la sauce fromage *artichokes in cheese sauce*
soupe à l'oignon *French onion soup*
tarte à l'oignon *onion tart*
ratatouille *courgettes, tomatoes, peppers, onions, aubergines*
pizzas *various pizzas*
crêpes *sweet and savoury pancakes with various fillings*
pâté végétal *vegetarian pâté*

■ EATING OUT

Are there any guided walks?
Y a-t-il des promenades guidées?
ee a-teel day promnad geeday

Do you have a guide to local walks?
Avez-vous un guide des promenades à faire dans la région?
avay vooz uñ geed day promnad a fehr doñ la ray-zhyoñ

Do you know any good walks?
Vous connaissez de bonnes promenades?
voo koneh-say duh bon promnad

How many kilometres is the walk?
La promenade fait combien de kilomètres?
la promnad feh koñ-byañ duh keelo-metr

How long will it take?
Ça prendra combien de temps?
sa proñ-dra koñ-byañ duh toñ

Is it very steep?
Est-ce que ça monte dur?
es kuh sa moñt door

We'd like to go climbing
Nous aimerions faire de l'escalade
nooz ehm-ryoñ fehr duh leska-lad

Do I/we need walking boots?
Est-ce qu'il faut des chaussures de marche?
es keel foh day shoh-soor duh marsh

Should we take...?
Est-ce qu'il faut emporter...?
es keel foh oñportay...

waterproofs
des imperméables
dayz añ-pehrmay-abl

water	food	a compass
de l'eau	quelque chose à manger	une boussole
duh loh	*kelkuh zhohz a moñ-zhay*	*oon boosol*

What time does it get dark?
À quelle heure est-ce qu'il commence à faire noir?
a kel ur es keel komoñs a fehr nwar

■ MAPS, GUIDES... ■ SIGHTSEEING & TOURIST OFFICE

BULLETIN MÉTÉOROLOGIQUE	WEATHER FORECAST
TEMPS VARIABLE	CHANGEABLE WEATHER
BEAU	FINE
TEMPS ORAGEUX	THUNDERY WEATHER
COUVERT	CLOUDY

It's sunny
Il fait du soleil
eel feh doo solay

It's raining
Il pleut
eel pluh

It's snowing
Il neige
eel nezh

It's windy
Il fait du vent
eel feh doo voñ

What a lovely day!
Quelle belle journée!
kel bel zhoornay

What awful weather!
Quel mauvais temps!
kel moveh toñ

What do you think the weather will be like tomorrow?
Quel temps croyez-vous qu'il fera demain?
kel toñ krwa-yay voo keel fuh-ra duhmañ

Do you think it's going to rain?
Vous croyez qu'il va pleuvoir?
voo krwa-yay keel va pluhvwar

Do I need an umbrella?
J'ai besoin d'un parapluie?
zhay buhzwañ duñ para-plwee

When will it stop raining?
Quand va-t-il arrêter de pleuvoir?
koñ vat-eel areh-tay duh pluhvwar

It's very hot
Il fait très chaud
eel feh treh shoh

Do you think there will be a storm?
Vous croyez qu'il va y avoir un orage?
voo krwa-yay keel va ee avwar uñ orazh

Do you think it will snow?
Vous pensez qu'il va neiger?
voo poñsay keel va neh-zhay

What is the temperature?
Quelle température fait-il?
kel toñpay-ratoor feh-teel

■ MAKING FRIENDS

The wine list, please
La carte des vins, s'il vous plaît
la kart day vañ seel voo pleh

red wine / white wine
du vin blanc / du vin rouge
doo vañ bloñ / doo vañ roozh

Can you recommend a good wine?
Pouvez-vous nous recommander un bon vin?
poovay voo noo ruhko-moñday uñ boñ vañ

A bottle...
Une bouteille...
oon bootay

A carafe...
Un pichet...
uñ pee-shay

of the house wine
de la cuvée du patron
duh la koovay doo patroñ

Barsac *sweet white wine*
Beaujolais *light fruity wines to be drunk young (Burgundy)*
Bergerac *red and white wines (Dordogne)*
Blanc de blancs *any white wine made from white grapes only*
Blanquette de Limoux *dry sparkling white wine (southwest)*
Bordeaux *region producing red (claret), dry and sweet wines*
Bourgueuil *light, fruity red wine to be drunk very young (Loire)*
Brouilly *among the finest Beaujolais: fruity, supple, full of flavour*
Cabernet Sauvignon *red wine with a slight blackcurrant aroma*
Cahors *dark, long-lived, powerful red wine from Massif Central*
Chablis *very dry, full-bodied white wine (Burgundy)*
Chambertin *one of the finest red Burgundies (Burgundy)*
Champagne *sparkling white/rosé (Champagne)*
Chardonnay *a white grape variety widely used in sparkling wines*
Châteauneuf-du-Pape *good, full-bodied red wine (Rhône)*
Côtes de Beaune *full-bodied red (Burgundy)*
Côtes du Rhône *full-bodied red (Rhône)*
Côtes du Roussillon *good ordinary red (Languedoc-Roussillon)*
Entre deux mers *medium-dry white wine from Bordeaux*
Fitou *dark red, sturdy wine (Languedoc-Roussillon)*
Gewürztraminer *fruity, spicy white wine (Alsace)*
Mâcon *good ordinary red and white wines (Burgundy)*
Médoc *principal wine-producing area of Bordeaux*
Mersault *dry white wine (Burgundy)*
Monbazillac *sweet white wine (Dordogne)*

CONT...

Muscadet *very dry white wine (Loire)*
Pouilly-Fuissé *light dry white wine (Burgundy)*
Pouilly-Fumé *spicy, dry white wine (Loire)*
Rosé d'Anjou *light, fruity rosé (Loire)*
Saint-Emilion *good full-bodied red wine (Bordeaux)*
Sancerre *dry white wine (Loire)*
Sauternes *sweet white wine (Bordeaux)*
Sylvaner *dry white wine (Alsace)*
Vouvray *dry, sweet and sparkling white wines (Loire)*

■ SPIRITS & LIQUEURS

What liqueurs do you have?
Qu'est-ce que vous avez comme liqueurs?
kes kuh vooz avay kom lee-kur

Armagnac *fine grape brandy from southwest France*
Calvados *apple brandy made from cider (Normandy)*
Cassis *blackcurrant liqueur:* **kir** *white wine and cassis apéritif*
Chartreuse *aromatic herb liqueur made by Carthusian monks*
Cognac *high quality white grape brandy*
Cointreau *orange-flavoured liqueur*
Crème de menthe *peppermint-flavoured liqueur*
Eau de vie *brandy (often made from plum, pear, etc.)*
Grand Marnier *tawny-coloured, orange-flavoured liqueur*
Izarra vert *green-coloured herb liqueur:* **jaune** *sweeter*
Kirsch *cherry-flavoured spirit from Alsace*
Mirabelle *plum spirit from Alsace*
Pastis *aniseed-based apéritif (like Pernod) to which water is added*

■ DRINKING ■ EATING OUT

What work do you do?
Qu'est-ce que vous faites comme travail?
kes kuh voo feht kom tra-vye

Do you enjoy it?
Ça vous plaît?
sa voo pleh

I'm...
Je suis...
zhuh swee...

a doctor	a manager	a secretary
médecin	directeur	secrétaire
maydsañ	*deerek-tur*	*suhkray-tehr*

I work in...
Je travaille dans...
zhuh tra-vye doñ...

a shop	a factory	the City
un magasin	une usine	les affaires
uñ maga-zañ	*oon oozeen*	*layz afehr*

I work from home
Je travaille à domicile
zhuh tra-vye a domee-seel

I'm self-employed
Je travaille à mon compte
zhuh tra-vye a moñ koñt

I have been unemployed for...
Je suis au chômage depuis...
zhuh swee oh shohmazh duhpwee...

months	years
mois	années
mwa	*anay*

It's very difficult to get a job at the moment
C'est très difficile de trouver un emploi en ce moment
say treh deefee-seel duh troovay uñ oñplwa oñ suh momoñ

What are your hours?
quelles heures faites-vous?
kel ur feht voo

I work from 9 to 5
Je travaille de 9 heures à 5 heures
zhuh tra-vye duh nuhf ur a sañk ur

from Monday to Friday
du lundi au vendredi
doo luñdee oh voñdruh-dee

How much holiday do you get?
Vous avez combien de vacances?
vooz avay koñ-byañ duh vakoñs

What do you want to be when you grow up?
Qu'est-ce que tu vas faire quand tu seras plus grand(e)?
kes kuh too va fehr koñ too suh-ra ploo groñ(d)

■ MAKING FRIENDS

93

NOUNS

Unlike English, French nouns have a gender: they are either masculine (**le**) or feminine (**la**). Therefore words for **the** and **a(n)** must agree with the noun they accompany – whether *masculine*, *feminine* or *plural*:

	masc.	*fem.*	*plural*
the	**le** chat	**la** rue	**les** chats, **les** rues
a, an	**un** chat	**une** rue	**des** chats, **des** rues

If the noun begins with a vowel (**a**, **e**, **i**, **o** or **u**) or an unsounded **h**, **le** and **la** shorten to **l'**, i.e. **l'avion** (*m*), **l'école** (*f*), **l'hôtel** (*m*).

NOTE: **le** and **les** used after the prepositions **à** (**to**, **at**) and **de** (**any**, **some**, **of**) contract as follows:

à + **le** = **au** (**au** cinéma but **à** <u>la</u> gare)

à + **les** = **aux** (**aux** magasins - applies to both (*m*) and (*f*))

de + **le** = **du** (**du** pain but **de** <u>la</u> confiture)

de + **les** = **des** (<u>des</u> pommes - applies to both (*m*) and (*f*))

There are some broad rules as to noun endings which indicate whether they are *masculine* or *feminine*:

Generally *masculine* endings: **-er**, **-ier**, **-eau**, **-t**, **-c**, **-age**, **-ail**, **-oir**, **-é**, **-on**, **-acle**, **-ège**, **-ème**, **-o**, **-ou**.

Generally *feminine* endings: **-euse**, **-trice**, **-ère**, **-ière**, **-elle**, **-te**, **-tte**, **-de**, **-che**, **-age**, **-aille**, **-oire**, **-ée**, **-té**, **-tié**, **-onne**, **-aison**, **-ion**, **-esse**, **-ie**, **-ine**, **-une**, **-ure**, **-ance**, **-anse**, **-ence**, **-ense**.

PLURALS

The general rule is to add an **s** to the singular:

> **le chat → les chats**

Exceptions occur with the following noun endings: **-eau**, **-eu**, **-al**

> **le bat<u>eau</u> → les bat<u>eaux</u>**
> **le nev<u>eu</u> → les nev<u>eux</u>**
> **le chev<u>al</u> → les chev<u>aux</u>**

Nouns ending in **s**, **x**, or **z** do not change in the plural.

> **le dos → les dos**
> **le prix → les prix**
> **le nez → les nez**

ADJECTIVES

Adjectives normally follow the noun they describe in French,
e.g.   **la pomme verte (the green apple)**

Some common exceptions which precede the noun are:
beau beautiful, **bon good**, **grand big**, **haut high**, **jeune young**,
long long, **joli pretty**, **mauvais bad**, **nouveau new**, **petit small**,
vieux old,

e.g.   **un bon livre (a good book)**

French adjectives have to reflect the gender of the noun they
describe. To make an adjective feminine, an **e** is added to the
masculine form (where this does not already end in an **e**, i.e.
jeune). A final consonant which is usually silent in the *masculine*
form is pronounced in the *feminine*:

masc. **le livre vert**   *fem.* **la pomme verte**
    luh leevr vehr   *la pom vehrt*
    (the green book)   **(the green apple)**

To make an adjective plural, an **s** is added to the singular form:
masculine plural – **verts** (remember – the ending is still silent:
vehr) or *feminine plural* – **vertes** (because of the **e**, the **t** ending
is sounded: *vehrt*).

MY, YOUR, HIS, HER

These words also depend on the gender and number of the
noun they accompany and not on the sex of the 'owner'.

	with masc. sing. noun	with fem. sing. noun	with plural nouns
my	mon	ma	mes
your (familiar, singular)	ton	ta	tes
his/her	son	sa	ses
our	notre	notre	nos
your (polite and plural)	votre	votre	vos
their	leur	leur	leurs

PRONOUNS

subject		*object*	
I	je, j'	me	me
you *(familiar)*	tu	you	te
you *(polite and plural)*	vous	you	vous
he/it	il	him/it	le, l'
she/it	elle	her/it	la, l'
we	nous	us	nous
they *(masc.)*	ils	them	les
they *(fem.)*	elles	them	les

In French there are two forms of **you** – **tu** and **vous**. **Tu** is the familiar form which is used with people you know well (friends and family). **Vous**, as well as being the plural form for **you**, is also the polite form of addressing someone. You should take care to use this form until the other person invites you to use the more familiar **tu**.

Object pronouns are placed before the verb,

e.g.   **il vous aime (he loves you)**
         nous la connaissons (we know her)

However, in commands or requests, object pronouns follow the verb,

e.g.   **écoutez-le (listen to him)**
         aidez-moi (help me)

NOTE: this does not apply to negative commands or requests,

e.g.   **ne le faites pas (don't do it)**

The object pronouns shown above are also used to mean **to me**, **to us**, etc. except:

         le and **la** become **lui (to him, to her)**
         les becomes **leur (to them)**,

e.g.   **il le lui donne (he gives it to him)**

VERBS

There are three main patterns of endings for verbs in French –
those ending -er, -ir and -re in the dictionary.

DON<u>NER</u>	TO GIVE
je donne	I give
tu donnes	you give
il/elle donne	he/she gives
nous donnons	we give
vous donnez	you give
ils/elles donnent	they give

FIN<u>IR</u>	TO FINISH
je finis	I finish
tu finis	you finish
il/elle finit	he/she finishes
nous finissons	we finish
vous finissez	you finish
ils/elles finissent	they finish

RÉPOND<u>RE</u>	TO REPLY
je réponds	I reply
tu réponds	you reply
il/elle répond	he/she replies
nous répondons	we reply
vous répondez	you reply
ils/elles répondent	they reply

IRREGULAR VERBS

Among the most important irregular verbs are the following:

ÊTRE	TO BE
je suis	I am
tu es	you are
il/elle est	he/she is
nous sommes	we are
vous êtes	you are
ils/elles sont	they are

AVOIR	TO HAVE
j'ai	I have
tu as	you have
il/elle a	he/she has
nous avons	we have
vous avez	you have
ils/elles ont	they have

ALLER	TO GO
je vais	I go
tu vas	you go
il/elle va	he/she goes
nous allons	we go
vous allez	you go
ils/elles vont	they go

POUVOIR	TO BE ABLE
je peux	I can
tu peux	you can
il/elle peut	he/she can
nous pouvons	we can
vous pouvez	you can
ils/elles peuvent	they can

PAST TENSE

To form the simple past tense, **I gave/I have given**, **I finished/I have finished**, combine the present tense of the verb **avoir – to have** with the past participle of the verb (**donné, fini, répondu**),

e.g.
j'ai donné   **I gave/I have given**
j'ai fini   **I finished/I have finished**
j'ai répondu   **I replied/I have replied**

Not all verbs take **avoir** (j'ai..., il a...) as their auxiliary verb; some verbs take **être** (je suis..., il est...). These are intransitive verbs (which have no object),

e.g.
je suis allé   **I went**
je suis né   **I was born**

When the auxiliary verb **être** is used, the past participle (**allé, né,** etc.) becomes adjectival and agrees with the subject of the verb,

e.g.
nous sommes allés   **we went** *(plural)*
je suis née   **I was born** *(female)*

a	un/une
abbey	l'abbaye (f)
about (approximately)	environ
(concerning)	au sujet de
above	au-dessus
accident	l'accident (m)
accommodation	le logement
accompany	accompagner
ache	la douleur
my head aches	j'ai mal à la tête
adaptor (electrical)	l'adaptateur (m)
address	l'adresse (f)
adhesive tape	le ruban adhésif
admission charge	l'entrée (f)
adult	l'adulte (m/f)
advance: in advance	à l'avance
advertisement	l'annonce (f) ; la publicité
advise	conseiller ; aviser
after	après
afternoon	l'après-midi (m)
aftershave	l'après-rasage (m)
again	de nouveau ; encore
against	contre
agency	l'agence (f)
agent	l'agent (m)
ago: a week ago	il y a une semaine
agree	être d'accord
AIDS	SIDA
air-conditioning	la climatisation
air mail	par avion
airport	l'aéroport (m)
aisle	le couloir
alarm	l'alarme (f)

alarm clock	le réveil
alcohol	l'alcool *(m)*
alcoholic	alcoolique
all	tout(e)/tous/toutes
allergic to	allergique à
allow	permettre
allowance *(customs)*	la quantité tolérée
all right *(agreed)*	d'accord
are you all right?	*ça va?*
almond	l'amande *(f)*
almost	presque
alone	tout(e) seul(e)
Alps	les Alpes
already	déjà
also	aussi
always	toujours
am	suis *(to be)* see **GRAMMAR**
ambulance	l'ambulance *(f)*
America	l'Amérique *(f)*
American	américain(e)
amount *(total)*	le montant
anaesthetic	l'anesthésique *(m)*
and	et
angry	fâché(e)
another	un(e) autre
another beer?	*encore une bière?*
answer *n*	la réponse
answer *vb*	répondre à
antibiotic	l'antibiotique *(m)*
antifreeze	l'antigel *(m)*
antiseptic	l'antiseptique *(m)*
any	de (du/de la/des) see **GRAMMAR**
have you any apples?	*avez-vous des pommes?*
apartment	l'appartement *(m)*

apéritif	l'apéritif (m)
appendicitis	l'appendicite (f)
apple	la pomme
appointment	le rendez-vous
approximately	à peu près
apricot	l'abricot (m)
are	sont (to be) see GRAMMAR
arm	le bras
arrange	arranger
arrival	l'arrivée (f)
arrive	arriver
art gallery	le musée d'art
arthritis	l'arthrite (f)
artichoke	l'artichaut (m)
ashtray	le cendrier
asparagus	les asperges (fpl)
aspirin	l'aspirine (f)
asthma	l'asthme (m)
at	à
at home	à la maison
attractive	attrayant(e)
aubergine	l'aubergine (f)
auction	la vente aux enchères
Australia	l'Australie (f)
Australian	australien(ne)
author	l'écrivain ; l'auteur (m)
automatic	automatique
autumn	l'automne (m)
available	disponible
avalanche	l'avalanche (f)
average	moyen(ne)
avoid	éviter
awful	affreux (-euse)

baby	le bébé
baby food	les petits pots (mpl)
babysitter	le/la babysitter
back (of body)	le dos
backpack	le sac à dos
back up (computer)	sauvegarder
bacon	le bacon
bad (food, weather)	mauvais(e)
bag	le sac
(suitcase)	la valise
baggage	les bagages (mpl)
baggage allowance	le poids (de bagages) autorisé
baggage reclaim	la livraison des bagages
bait (for fishing)	l'appât (m)
baker's	la boulangerie
balcony	le balcon
ball	la balle
banana	la banane
band (musical)	l'orchestre (m)
bandage	le pansement
bank	la banque
bank account	le compte en banque
bankrupt (to go)	faire faillite
bar	le bar
barber	le coiffeur
bargain n (good buy)	l'affaire (f)
bargain vb	négocier
basket	le panier
bath	le bain
to take a bath	prendre un bain
bathing cap	le bonnet de bain
bathroom	la salle de bains
battery (for car)	la batterie
(for radio, etc.)	la pile

be	être **(to be)** see **GRAMMAR**
beach	la plage
bean	le haricot
beautiful	beau (belle)
because	parce que
become	devenir
bed	le lit
bedding	la literie
bedroom	la chambre à coucher
beef	le bœuf
beer	la bière
beetroot	la betterave
before	avant
begin	commencer
behave	se comporter
behind	derrière
Belgian	belge
Belgium	la Belgique
believe	croire
below	sous
belt	la ceinture
beside	à côté de
best	le/la mieux
bet	le pari
better	meilleur(e)
between	entre
beware of	prendre garde de
beyond	au-delà de
bicycle	la bicyclette ; le vélo
big	grand(e)
bigger (than)	plus grand(e) (que)
bill	l'addition *(f)* ; la note ; la facture
bin	la poubelle

binoculars	les jumelles *(fpl)*
bird	l'oiseau *(m)*
birthday	l'anniversaire *(m)*
happy birthday!	*bon anniversaire!*
birthday card	la carte d'anniversaire
bit: *a bit (of)*	un peu (de)
bitten	mordu(e)
(by insect)	piqué(e)
bitter	amer (-ère)
black	noir(e)
blackcurrant	le cassis
blame	la faute
blank *(on form)*	en blanc
blanket	la couverture
bleach	l'eau *(f)* de Javel
blocked	bouché(e)
blood	le sang
blood group	le groupe sanguin
blouse	le chemisier
blow-dry	le brushing
blue	bleu(e)
board (of directors)	le conseil (d'administration)
boarding card	la carte d'embarquement
boarding house	la pension (de famille)
boat	le bateau
boat trip	l'excursion *(f)* en bateau
body	le corps
boiled	bouilli(e)
book *n*	le livre
book *vb*	réserver
booking	la réservation
booking office	le guichet de location
book of tickets	le carnet de tickets

bookshop	la librairie
boots *(to wear)*	les bottes *(fpl)*
border	la frontière
borrow	emprunter
boss	le chef
both	les deux
bottle	la bouteille
bottle opener	l'ouvre-bouteilles *(m)*
box	la boîte
box office	le bureau de location
boy	le garçon
boyfriend	le petit ami
bra	le soutien-gorge
bracelet	le bracelet
brake fluid	le liquide pour freins
brakes	les freins *(mpl)*
branch *(of bank, etc.)*	l'agence *(f)*
brand *(make)*	la marque
brandy	le cognac
brave	courageux (-euse)
bread	le pain
break	casser
breakable	fragile
breakdown	la panne
breakdown van	la dépanneuse
breakfast	le petit déjeuner
breast *(chicken)*	le blanc
briefcase	la serviette
brick	la brique
bring	apporter
Britain	la Grande Bretagne
British	britannique
brochure	la brochure

broken	cassé(e)
broken down (car, etc.)	en panne
brooch	la broche
broom	le balai
brother	le frère
brown	marron
brush	la brosse
Brussels sprouts	les choux (mpl) de Bruxelles
bucket	le seau
budget	le budget
buffet	le buffet
buffet car	la voiture-buffet
build	construire
building (offices, flats)	l'immeuble (m)
building site	le chantier
bulb (light)	l'ampoule (f)
burn	brûler
bus	l'autobus (m)
business	les affaires (fpl)
business card	la carte de visite
business class	la classe affaires
business trip	le voyage d'affaires
bus station	la gare routière
bus stop	l'arrêt (m) d'autobus
busy	occupé(e)
but	mais
butcher's	la boucherie
butter	le beurre
button	le bouton
buy	acheter
by (via)	via
(beside)	à côté de
bypass	la rocade

cabaret	le cabaret
cabbage	le chou
cablecar	le téléphérique ; la benne
café	le café
cake	le gâteau
call *vb*	appeler
call *n (on telephone)*	l'appel *(m)*
calm	calme
camcorder	le caméscope
camera	l'appareil photo *(m)*
camp	camper
campsite	le camping
can *n*	la boîte
can *vb (to be able)*	pouvoir *see* **GRAMMAR**
can I ...?	puis-je ...?
Canada	le Canada
Canadian	canadien(ne)
cancel	annuler
cancellation	l'annulation *(f)*
canoe	le canoë
canoeing	le (sport du) canoë
can opener	l'ouvre-boîtes *(m)*
car	la voiture
carafe	le pichet
caravan	la caravane
carburettor	le carburateur
card	la carte
careful *(to be)*	faire attention à
car hire	la location de voitures
car park	le parking
carpet	le tapis
carriage *(railway)*	la voiture
carrot	la carotte

carry	porter
car wash	le lave-auto
case *(suitcase)*	la valise
cash *vb (cheque)*	encaisser
cash *n*	l'argent *(m)* liquide
cash desk	la caisse
cashier	le caissier/la caissière
casino	le casino
cassette	la cassette
castle	le château
cat	le chat
catch *(bus, train)*	prendre
cathedral	la cathédrale
Catholic	catholique
cauliflower	le chou-fleur
cave	la grotte
ceiling	le plafond
celery	le céleri
cemetery	le cimetière
centimetre	le centimètre
central	central(e)
centre	le centre
century	le siècle
cereal *(for breakfast)*	les céréales *(fpl)*
certain *(sure)*	certain(e)
certificate	le certificat
chain	la chaîne
chair	la chaise
chairlift	le télésiège
chalet	le chalet
Champagne	le Champagne
change *n (money)*	la monnaie
change *vb*	changer

changing room	la cabine d'essayage
chapel	la chapelle
charge	le prix
cheap	bon marché
cheaper	moins cher
check	vérifier
check in	enregistrer
check-in desk	l'enregistrement (m) des bagages
cheerio	au revoir
cheers!	à la vôtre!
cheese	le fromage
chemist's	la pharmacie
cheque	le chèque
cheque book	le carnet de chèques
cheque card	la carte d'identité bancaire
cherry	la cerise
chestnut	la châtaigne
chewing gum	le chewing-gum
chicken	le poulet
chickenpox	la varicelle
child	l'enfant (m)
children	les enfants
chilli	le piment rouge
chips	les frites (fpl)
chocolate	le chocolat
chocolates	les chocolats
Christmas	Noël (m/f)
merry Christmas!	joyeux Noël!
church	l'église (f)
cider	le cidre
cigar	le cigare
cigarette	la cigarette
cinema	le cinéma

circus	le cirque
city	la ville
clean *adj*	propre
clean *vb*	nettoyer
cleanser *(for face)*	le démaquillant
client	le client/la cliente
climbing	l'escalade *(f)*
climbing boots	les chaussures *(fpl)* d'escalade
cloakroom	le vestiaire
clock	l'horloge *(f)*
close *adj (near)*	proche
close *vb*	fermer
closed	fermé(e)
cloth	le chiffon
clothes	les vêtements *(mpl)*
clothes peg	la pince à linge
cloudy	nuageux (-euse)
cloves	les clous *(mpl)* de girofle
club	le club
coach *(bus)*	le car ; l'autocar *(m)*
(train)	la voiture
coach trip	l'excursion *(f)* en car
coast	la côte
coastguard	le garde-côte
coat	le manteau
coat hanger	le cintre
cocktail	le cocktail
cocoa	le cacao
coconut	la noix de coco
coffee	le café
white coffee	le café au lait
black coffee	le café noir
coin	la pièce de monnaie
Coke®	le Coca(-cola)®

colander	la passoire
cold	froid
I'm cold	j'ai froid
I have a cold	j'ai un rhume
collect (someone)	aller chercher
colour	la couleur
comb	le peigne
come	venir
(to come back)	revenir
(to come in)	entrer
come in!	entrez!
comfortable	confortable
communion	la communion
company	la compagnie
compartment	le compartiment
competitor	le/la concurrent(e)
complain	se plaindre
compulsory	obligatoire
computer	l'ordinateur (m)
concert	le concert
condensed milk	le lait condensé
conditioner	l'après-shampooing (m)
condom	le préservatif
conductor (on bus)	le receveur
conference	la conférence
confession	la confession
confirm	confirmer
congratulations	félicitations!
connection	la correspondance
conserve	préserver
consider	considérer
consign	expédier
constipated	constipé(e)
consulate	le consulat

contact vb	contacter
contact lenses	les verres (mpl) de contact
contraceptive	le contraceptif
contract	le contrat
cook	le cuisinier/la cuisinière
cooker	la cuisinière
cool	frais (fraîche)
copy n	la copie
copy vb	copier
corkscrew	le tire-bouchon
corner	le coin
cornflakes	les cornflakes
cortisone	la cortisone
cosmetics	les produits (mpl) de beauté
cost	le coût
costs (expenses)	les frais (mpl)
cotton	le coton
cotton wool	le coton hydrophile
couchette	la couchette
cough	la toux
count (add up)	compter
country (not town)	la campagne
(nation)	le pays
couple (two people)	le couple
courgette	la courgette
courier	le guide
course (of meal)	le plat
cover charge	le couvert
cow	la vache
crab	le crabe
crash (car)	l'accident (m)
crash helmet	le casque protecteur
crazy	fou (folle)

cream	la crème
credit card	la carte de crédit
crisis	la crise
crisps	les chips (mpl)
croquette	la croquette
cross (road)	traverser
crossing (by sea)	la traversée
crossroads	le carrefour ; le croisement
crowd	la foule
crowded	bondé(e)
crown	la couronne
cruise	la croisière
crumb	la miette
cucumber	le concombre
cup	la tasse
cupboard	le placard
currant	le raisin sec
currency	la devise ; la monnaie
current	le courant
cursor (computer)	le curseur
curtain	le rideau
curve (in road)	le virage
cushion	le coussin
custard	la crème anglaise
custom (tradition)	l'usage (m) ; la coutume
customary	habituel (-elle)
customer	le/la client(e)
customs	la douane
cut n	la coupure
cut vb	couper
cutlery	les couverts (mpl)
cycle	le vélo ; la bicyclette
cycling	le cyclisme

daily *(each day)*	tous les jours
damage n	les dégâts *(mpl)*
damp	humide
dance n	le bal
dance vb	danser
dangerous	dangereux (-euse)
dark *(colour)*	foncé(e)
date	la date
date of birth	la date de naissance
daughter	la fille
day	le jour
dear	cher (chère)
decaffeinated	décaféiné(e)
deck chair	la chaise longue
declare	déclarer
deep	profond(e)
deep freeze	le congélateur
defrost	dégivrer
de-ice	dégivrer
delay	le retard
delicious	délicieux (-euse)
dentist	le/la dentiste
dentures	le dentier
deodorant	le déodorant
department store	le grand magasin
departure	le départ
departure lounge	la salle de départ
deposit	les arrhes *(fpl)*
dessert	le dessert
details	les détails *(mpl)*
detergent	le détergent
detour	la déviation
develop	développer

diabetic	diabétique
dialling code	l'indicatif (m)
dialling tone	la tonalité
diamond	le diamant
diarrhoea	la diarrhée
diary	l'agenda (m)
dictionary	le dictionnaire
diesel	le gas-oil
diet	le régime
different	différent(e)
difficult	difficile
dinghy	le youyou
dining room	la salle à manger
dinner	le dîner
direct (train, etc.)	direct(e)
directory	l'annuaire (m)
dirty	sale
disabled	handicapé(e)
disco	la discothèque
discount	le rabais
discover	découvrir
disease	la maladie
dish	le plat
dishwasher	le lave-vaisselle
disinfectant	le désinfectant
distant	lointain(e)
distilled water	l'eau (f) distillée
disturb	déranger
divorced	divorcé(e)
dizzy	pris(e) de vertige
do	faire
doctor	le médecin
documents	les papiers (mpl)

doll	la poupée
dollar	le dollar
door	la porte
double	double
double bed	le grand lit
double room	la chambre pour deux personnes
doughnut	le beignet
down *(go downstairs)*	descendre
downstairs	en bas
draught	le courant d'air
dress *n*	la robe
dress *vb*	s'habiller
dressing *(for food)*	la vinaigrette
drink *n*	la boisson
drink *vb*	boire
drinking chocolate	le chocolat chaud
drinking water	l'eau *(f)* potable
drive	conduire
driver *(of car)*	le conducteur ; la conductrice
driving licence	le permis de conduire
drunk	ivre
dry *adj*	sec (sèche)
dry *vb*	sécher
dry-cleaner's	le pressing
duck	le canard
dummy	la sucette ; la tétine
during	pendant
dust	la poussière
duty-free	hors taxe
duty-free shop	la boutique hors taxe
duvet	la couette
dye	la teinture
dynamo	la dynamo

each	chacun/chacune
ear	l'oreille (f)
earlier	plus tôt
early	tôt
earn	gagner
earrings	les boucles (fpl) d'oreille
earth	la terre
earthquake	le tremblement de terre
east	l'est (m)
Easter	Pâques (m or fpl)
easy	facile
eat	manger
edition	l'édition (f)
eel	l'anguille (f)
efficient (person)	capable
egg	l'œuf (m)
fried eggs	les œufs sur le plat
hard-boiled egg	l'œuf dur
scrambled eggs	les œufs brouillés
either: either one	l'un ou l'autre
elastic band	l'élastique (m)
electric	électrique
electrician	l'électricien (m)
electricity	l'électricité (f)
electricity meter	le compteur d'électricité
electric razor	le rasoir électrique
embassy	l'ambassade (f)
emergency	l'urgence (f)
empty	vide
end	la fin
engaged (to be married)	fiancé(e)
(toilet, phone)	occupé(e)
engine	le moteur
England	l'Angleterre (f)

English	anglais(e)
enjoy oneself	s'amuser
enormous	énorme
enough	assez
enquiry desk	les renseignements (mpl)
entertainment	les divertissements (mpl)
entrance	l'entrée (f)
entrance fee	le prix d'entrée
envelope	l'enveloppe (f)
environment	le milieu ; l'environnement (m)
equal	égal(e)
equipment	l'équipement (m)
error	l'erreur (f)
escalator	l'escalator (m)
escape	échapper
especially	surtout
essential	indispensable
establish	établir ; fonder
eurocheque	l'eurochèque (m)
Europe	l'Europe (f)
evening	le soir
in the evening	le soir
evening meal	le dîner
event	l'événement
every	chaque
everyone	tout le monde
everything	tout
excellent	excellent(e)
except	sauf
excess luggage	l'excédent (m) de bagages
exchange n	l'échange (m)
exchange vb	échanger
exchange rate	le taux de change

exciting	passionnant(e)
excursion	l'excursion (f)
excuse: *excuse me!*	*excusez-moi!*
exhaust pipe	le pot d'échappement
exhibition	l'exposition (f)
exist	exister
exit	la sortie
expensive	cher (chère)
expert	l'expert(e) (m/f)
expire *(ticket, passport)*	expirer
explain	expliquer
express n *(train)*	le rapide
express adj *(parcel, etc.)*	par exprès
extension *(electrical)*	la rallonge
extra *(additional)*	supplémentaire
eye	l'œil (m)
eyes	les yeux (mpl)
face	le visage
facilities	les installations (fpl)
factory	l'usine (f)
fail	échouer
faint	s'évanouir
fainted	évanoui(e)
fair *(just)*	juste
(funfair)	la fête foraine
fall vb	tomber
family	la famille
famous	célèbre
fan *(handheld)*	l'éventail (m)
(electric)	le ventilateur
fan belt	la courroie de ventilateur
far	loin

fare (bus, metro, etc.)	le prix du ticket
farm	la ferme
fast	rapide
fasten	attacher
fat	gros (grosse)
father	le père
fault: *it's not my fault*	*ce n'est pas de ma faute*
favour	le service
favourite	préféré(e)
fear	la peur
feather	la plume
fee	les honoraires (mpl)
feed	nourrir
feel	sentir
ferry	le ferry
festival	le festival
fetch	aller chercher
fever	la fièvre
few: *a few*	*un peu (de ...)*
fiancé(e)	le fiancé/la fiancée
field	le champ
fig	la figue
file (computer)	le fichier
fill	remplir
fill it up!	*le plein!*
fillet	le filet
filling	le plombage
film	le film
(for camera)	la pellicule
filter	le filtre
filter-tipped	à bout filtre
find	trouver
finger	le doigt
finish	finir

finished	fini(e)
fire	le feu ; l'incendie (f)
fire brigade	les pompiers (mpl)
fire extinguisher	l'extincteur (m)
fireplace	la cheminée
firework	le feu d'artifice
firm	la compagnie
first	premier (-ière)
first aid	les premiers soins (mpl)
first class	en première
first floor	le premier étage
first name	le prénom
fish n	le poisson
fish vb	pêcher
fit : it doesn't fit me	ça ne me va pas
fit n (medical)	l'attaque (f)
fix	fixer
fizzy	gazeux (-euse)
flag	le drapeau
flame	la flamme
flash	le flash
flask	le thermos
flat (apartment)	l'appartement (m)
flat tyre	la crevaison
flavour	le goût
(ice cream)	le parfum
flesh	la chair
flight	le vol
flippers	les palmes (fpl)
floor (of building)	l'étage (m)
(of room)	le plancher
floppy disk	la disquette
flour	la farine
flower	la fleur

flu n	la grippe
fly n	la mouche
fly vb (bird, etc)	voler
(person)	voyager en avion
fly sheet	le double toit
focus (camera)	mettre au point
fog	le brouillard
foil	le papier alu(minium)
fold vb	plier
follow	suivre
font (typeface)	la police
food	la nourriture
food poisoning	l'intoxication (f) alimentaire
foot	le pied
football	le football
for (in exchange for)	pour
forbidden	interdit(e)
foreign	étranger (-ère)
forest	la forêt
forever	toujours
forget	oublier
fork	la fourchette
(in road)	l'embranchement (m)
form	le formulaire ; la formule ; la fiche
fortnight	la quinzaine
forward	en avant
foul (football)	la faute
fountain	la fontaine
fowl	la volaille
fox	le renard
fragrance	le parfum
frame (picture)	le cadre
France	la France

ENGLISH-FRENCH — F

free *(not occupied)*	libre
(costing nothing)	gratuit(e)
freedom	la liberté
freezer	le congélateur
French	français(e)
French beans	les haricots verts *(mpl)*
frequent	fréquent(e)
fresh	frais (fraîche)
fridge	le frigo
fried	frit(e)
friend	l'ami/l'amie
fright	l'effroi *(m)* ; la peur
frog	la grenouille
from	de
front	le devant
frost	le gel
frozen *(food)*	surgelé(e)
fruit	le fruit
fruit juice	le jus de fruit
fruit salad	la salade de fruits
frying-pan	la poêle
fuel	le combustible
fuel pump	la pompe d'alimentation
full	plein(e)
full board	la pension complète
fully	complètement
funfair	la fête foraine
funny *(amusing)*	amusant(e)
(strange)	curieux (-euse)
fur	la fourrure
furnished	meublé(e)
furniture	les meubles *(mpl)*
fuse	le fusible
future	l'avenir *(m)*

gallery	la galerie
gallon	= *approx. 4.5 litres*
game	le jeu
garage	le garage
garden	le jardin
garlic	l'ail *(m)*
gas cylinder	la bouteille de gaz
gear	la vitesse
gentleman	le monsieur
gents	les toilettes *(fpl)*
genuine	authentique
German	allemand(e)
Germany	l'Allemagne *(f)*
get *(obtain)*	obtenir
(fetch)	aller chercher
(get in vehicle)	monter
(get off bus, etc.)	descendre
gift	le cadeau
gift shop	la boutique de souvenirs
ginger	le gingembre
girl	la fille
girlfriend	la petite amie
give	donner
glass	le verre
glasses	les lunettes *(fpl)*
gloves	les gants *(mpl)*
glue	la colle
go	aller
(go back)	retourner
(go downstairs, etc.)	descendre
(go in)	entrer
(go out ; leave)	sortir
goggles *(for swimming)*	les lunettes *(fpl)* protectrices
gold	l'or *(m)*

golf course	le terrain de golf
good	bon (bonne)
good afternoon	bonjour
goodbye	au revoir
good evening	bonsoir
good morning	bonjour
good night	bonne nuit
goose	l'oie (f)
gramme	le gramme
grandfather	le grand-père
grandmother	la grand-mère
grapefruit	le pamplemousse
grapes	le raisin
grass	l'herbe (f)
greasy	gras (grasse)
green	vert(e)
green card (insurance)	la carte verte
grey	gris(e)
grilled	grillé(e)
grocer's	l'épicerie (f)
ground	la terre ; le sol
ground floor	le rez-de-chaussée
groundsheet	le tapis de sol
group	le groupe
guarantee	la garantie
guard (on train)	le chef de train
guest (house guest)	l'invité(e) (m/f)
(in hotel)	le/la client(e)
guesthouse	la pension
guide	le guide
guidebook	le guide
guided tour	la visite guidée
gym shoes	les chaussures de tennis/de sport

haemorrhoids	les hémorroïdes *(fpl)*
hair	les cheveux *(mpl)*
hairbrush	la brosse à cheveux
haircut	la coupe (de cheveux)
hairdresser *(male)*	le coiffeur
(female)	la coiffeuse
hairdryer	le sèche-cheveux
hairgrip	la pince à cheveux
hair spray	la laque
half	la moitié
a half bottle of ...	*une demi-bouteille de ...*
half board	la demi-pension
half fare	le demi-tarif
halfway	à mi-chemin
ham	le jambon
hand	la main
handbag	le sac à main
handicapped	handicapé(e)
handkerchief	le mouchoir
handle	la poignée
hand luggage	les bagages *(mpl)* à main
hand-made	fait main
handsome	beau (belle)
hangover	la gueule de bois
hang up *(telephone)*	raccrocher
happen	arriver ; se passer
what happened?	*qu'est-ce qui s'est passé?*
happy	heureux (-euse)
harbour	le port
hard	dur(e)
hare	le lièvre
harm *n*	le mal
harm *vb*	faire du mal
harvest *(grapes)*	les vendanges *(fpl)*

hat	le chapeau
have	avoir *see* GRAMMAR
hay fever	le rhume des foins
hazelnut	la noisette
he	il *see* GRAMMAR
head	la tête
headache	le mal de tête
head waiter	le maître d'hôtel
hear	entendre
heart	le cœur
heart attack	la crise cardiaque
heater	l'appareil *(m)* de chauffage
heating	le chauffage
heat up *(milk, water)*	chauffer
heavy	lourd(e)
heel	le talon
height	la hauteur
hello	bonjour
(on telephone)	allô
help *n*	l'aide *(f)*
help!	au secours!
help *vb*	aider
hem	l'ourlet *(m)*
herb	l'herbe *(f)*
here	ici
hide	cacher
high	haut(e)
high blood pressure	la tension
high chair	la chaise haute
high tide	la marée haute
hill	la colline
hill-walking	la randonnée de basse montagne
hire	louer
hit	frapper

hitchhike	faire du stop
hold	tenir
(contain)	contenir
hold-up *(traffic jam)*	l'embouteillage *(m)*
hole	le trou
holiday	les vacances *(fpl)*
on holiday	en vacances
home	la maison
homesick *(to be)*	avoir le mal du pays
honey	le miel
honeymoon	la lune de miel
hook *(fishing)*	l'hameçon *(m)*
hope	espérer
I hope so/not	j'espère que oui/non
hors d'œuvre	le hors d'œuvre
horse	le cheval
hose	le tuyau
hospital	l'hôpital *(m)*
hot	chaud(e)
I'm hot	j'ai chaud
it's hot *(weather)*	il fait chaud
hotel	l'hôtel *(m)*
hour	l'heure *(f)*
house	la maison
house wine	la réserve du patron
hovercraft	l'aéroglisseur *(m)*
how? *(in what way)*	comment?
how much/many?	combien?
how are you?	comment allez-vous?
hungry *(to be)*	avoir faim
hurry: I'm in a hurry	je suis pressé
hurt : my back hurts	j'ai mal au dos
husband	le mari
hydrofoil	l'hydrofoil *(m)*

I	je *see* **GRAMMAR**
ice	la glace
(cube)	le glaçon
ice cream	la glace
iced	glacé(e)
ice lolly	l'esquimau (m)
ice rink	la patinoire
idea	l'idée (f)
if	si
ignition	l'allumage (m)
ill	malade
illness	la maladie
immediately	immédiatement
important	important(e)
impossible	impossible
improve	améliorer
in	dans
inch	= *approx. 2.5 cm*
included	compris(e)
income	le revenu
increase	augmenter
indigestion	l'indigestion (f)
indoors	à l'intérieur
infectious	infectieux (-euse)
information	les renseignements (mpl)
information office	le bureau de renseignements
injection	la piqûre
injured	blessé(e)
ink	l'encre (f)
insect	l'insecte (m)
insect bite	la piqûre (d'insecte)
insect repellent	l'anti-insecte (m)
insert	insérer

inside	l'intérieur *(m)*
inside the car	*dans la voiture*
instant coffee	le café instantané
instead of	au lieu de
instructor	le moniteur/la monitrice
insulin	l'insuline *(f)*
insurance	l'assurance *(f)*
insurance certificate	la carte d'assurance *(f)*
insured	assuré(e)
intend to	avoir l'intention de
interesting	intéressant(e)
international	international(e)
interpreter	l'interprète *(m/f)*
interval *(theatre)*	l'entracte *(m)*
interview	l'entrevue *(f)*
(TV, etc.)	l'interview *(f)*
into	dans
introduce	présenter
invitation	l'invitation *(f)*
invite	inviter
invoice	la facture
Ireland	l'Irlande *(f)*
Irish	irlandais(e)
iron n *(for clothes)*	le fer
iron vb	repasser
ironmonger's	la quincaillerie
is	est **(to be)** see GRAMMAR
island	l'île *(f)*
it	il/elle see GRAMMAR
Italian	italien(ne)
Italy	l'Italie *(f)*
item	l'article *(m)*
itemized bill	la facture détaillée

jack (for car)	le cric
jacket	la veste
jam (food)	la confiture
jammed	coincé(e)
Japan	le Japon
jar (glass)	le bocal
jaw	la mâchoire
jazz	le jazz
jealous	jaloux (-ouse)
jeans	le jean
jelly (dessert)	la gelée
jellyfish	la méduse
jetty (landing pier)	l'embarcadère (m)
jeweller's	la bijouterie
jewellery	les bijoux (mpl)
Jewish	juif (juive)
job	le travail
jog	faire du jogging
join	joindre
(become member)	devenir membre de
joint (body)	l'articulation (f)
joint venture	l'entreprise (f) en participation
joke	la plaisanterie
journalist	le/la journaliste
journey	le voyage
judge	le juge
jug	le pichet
juice	le jus
jump vb	sauter
jump leads	les câbles (mpl) de raccordement de batterie
junction (road)	le croisement ; le carrefour
just: just two	deux seulement
I've just arrived	je viens d'arriver

keep (retain)	garder
kennels	le chenil
kettle	la bouilloire
key	la clé
keyboard	le clavier
key in	introduire au clavier
keystroke	la frappe
kick	le coup de pied
kidneys (as food)	les rognons (mpl)
kill	tuer
kilo	le kilo
kilometre	le kilomètre
kind n (sort, type)	la sorte
kind adj (person)	gentil (-ille)
kiosk	le kiosque
kiss n	le baiser
kiss vb	embrasser
kitchen	la cuisine
kitten	le chaton
knee	le genou
knife	le couteau
knit	tricoter
knitting	le tricot
knock (on door)	frapper
knock down	faire tomber
(by car)	renverser
knot	le nœud
know (facts)	savoir
(be acquainted with)	connaître
knowledge	la connaissance

label	l'étiquette (f)
lace	la dentelle
ladder	l'échelle (f)
ladies	les toilettes (fpl) dames
lady	la dame
lager	la bière blonde
lake	le lac
lamb	l'agneau (m)
lamp	la lampe
land	la terre
landing (aircraft)	l'atterrissage (m)
lane	la ruelle
(of motorway)	la voie
language	la langue
large	grand(e)
last	dernier (-ière)
last week	la semaine dernière
late	tard
the train is late	le train a du retard
later	plus tard
laugh vb	rire
launderette	la laverie automatique
laundry service	le service de blanchisserie
lavatory	les toilettes (fpl)
lawyer	l'avocat(e) (m/f)
laxative	le laxatif
layby	l'aire (f) de stationnement
lazy	paresseux (-euse)
lead (electric)	le fil
(dog)	la laisse
leader (of group)	le chef de groupe
leak (of gas, liquid)	la fuite
(in roof)	la fuite
learn	apprendre

least: *at least*	au moins
leather	le cuir
leave	partir
(leave behind)	laisser
leek	le poireau
left	la gauche
on/to the left	*à gauche*
left-luggage (office)	la consigne
leg	la jambe
legal	légal(e)
leisure	le loisir
lemon	le citron
lemonade	la limonade
lemon tea	le thé au citron
lend	prêter
length	la longueur
lens	l'objectif *(m)*
Lent	le Carême
less (than)	moins (de)
lessen	diminuer
lesson	la leçon
let *(allow)*	permettre
(hire out)	louer
letter	la lettre
lettuce	la laitue
level-crossing	le passage à niveau
liable	responsable
library	la bibliothèque
licence	le permis
lid	le couvercle
lie down	se coucher ; s'allonger
lifeboat	le canot de sauvetage
lifeguard	le surveillant de plage
life jacket	le gilet de sauvetage

lift	l'ascenseur *(m)*
lift pass *(on ski slopes)*	l'abonnement *(m)* aux remontées
light	la lumière
have you a light?	*avez-vous du feu?*
light bulb	l'ampoule *(f)*
lighter	le briquet
lighthouse	le phare
lightning	l'éclair *(m)*
like *prep*	comme
like this	*comme ça*
like *vb*	aimer
I like coffee	*j'aime le café*
lime *(fruit)*	le citron vert
line	la ligne
linen	le lin
lion	le lion
lip-reading	la lecture sur les lèvres
lip salve	le baume pour les lèvres
lipstick	le rouge à lèvres
liqueur	la liqueur
list *n*	la liste
listen (to)	écouter
litre	le litre
litter	les ordures *(fpl)*
little	petit(e)
a little ...	*un peu de ...*
live	vivre ; habiter
I live in London	*j'habite (à) Londres*
liver	le foie
living room	la salle de séjour
loaf	le pain
lobster	le homard
local *(wine, speciality)*	local(e)
lock *n* *(on door, box)*	la serrure

lock vb (door)	**fermer à clé**
lollipop	**la sucette**
London	**Londres**
long	**long(ue)**
for a long time	longtemps
look	**regarder**
(to look after)	garder
(to look for)	chercher
loose (not fastened)	**desserré(e)**
lorry	**le camion**
lose	**perdre**
lost (object)	**perdu(e)**
I've lost ...	j'ai perdu ...
lost property office	**le bureau des objets trouvés**
lot: a lot	**beaucoup**
lotion	**la lotion**
loud	**fort(e)**
lounge (in hotel)	**le salon**
love (person)	**aimer**
I love swimming	j'aime nager
lovely	**charmant(e)**
low	**bas (basse)**
lower	**baisser**
low tide	**la marée basse**
luck	**la chance**
luggage	**les bagages** (mpl)
luggage allowance	**le poids maximum autorisé**
luggage rack	**le porte-bagages**
luggage tag	**l'étiquette** (f) **à bagages**
luggage trolley	**le chariot (à bagages)**
lunch	**le déjeuner**
lung	**le poumon**
Luxembourg	**Luxembourg** (m)
luxury	**de luxe**

machine	la machine
mad	fou (folle)
madam	madame
magazine	la revue
magnet	l'aimant (m)
magnifying glass	la loupe
magpie	la pie
maid	la domestique
main	principal(e)
main course	le plat de résistance
mains (electric)	le secteur
maintain	maintenir
make	faire
make-up	le maquillage
mallet	le maillet
man	l'homme (m)
manage	diriger ; gérer
manager	le directeur/la directrice
manner	la manière
manufacture	fabriquer
many	beaucoup
map	la carte ; le plan
marathon	le marathon
margarine	la margarine
mark	la marque
(stain)	la tache
market	le marché
marmalade	la confiture d'oranges
married	marié(e)
marsh	le marais
marvellous	merveilleux (-euse)
marzipan	la pâte d'amandes
mass (in church)	la messe

mass-produced	fabriqué(e) en série
mat	le tapis
match	l'allumette (f)
(game)	la partie
material *(cloth)*	le tissu
matter	importer
it doesn't matter	ça ne fait rien
what's the matter?	qu'est-ce qu'il y a?
mayonnaise	la mayonnaise
meadow	le pré
meal	le repas
mean *(signify)*	signifier
what does this mean?	qu'est-ce que cela signifie?
measles	la rougeole
meat	la viande
mechanic	le mécanicien
medical insurance	l'assurance (f) maladie
medicine	le médicament
medium	à point
meet	rencontrer
meeting	la réunion
melon	le melon
melt	fondre
member *(of club, etc.)*	le membre
memory	la mémoire
menu	le menu
meringue	la meringue
message	le message
metal	le métal
meter	le compteur
metre	le mètre
migraine	la migraine
mild	doux (douce)
mile	*8 km = approx. 5 miles*

milk	le lait
milkshake	le milk-shake
millimetre	le millimètre
million	le million
mince	la viande hachée
mind: do you mind if I...?	est-ce que cela vous gêne si je...?
mineral water	l'eau (f) minérale
minimum	le minimum
minister (church)	le pasteur
minor road	la route secondaire
mint (herb)	la menthe
(sweet)	le bonbon à la menthe
minus	moins
minute	la minute
mirror	la glace
miserable	malheureux (-euse)
miss (train, etc.)	manquer
Miss	Mademoiselle
missing	disparu(e)
mistake	l'erreur (f)
misty	brumeux (-euse)
misunderstanding	le malentendu
there must be a misunderstanding	il doit y avoir méprise
mix	mélanger
modern	moderne
moisturizer	le lait hydratant
mole	la taupe
monastery	le monastère
money	l'argent (m)
money order	le mandat
month	le mois
monthly	mensuel (-elle)

monument	le monument
moon	la lune
mop *(for floor)*	le balai à laver
more (than)	plus (de)
more wine	encore du vin
morning	le matin
mortgage	l'emprunt-logement (m)
mosquito	le moustique
most	le plus
moth *(clothes)*	la mite
mother	la mère
motor	le moteur
motor boat	le bateau à moteur
motor cycle	la moto
motorway	l'autoroute (f)
mountain	la montagne
mouse	la souris
mousse	la mousse
mouth	la bouche
move	bouger
Mr	Monsieur
Mrs	Madame
Ms	Madame
much	beaucoup
too much	trop
mumps	les oreillons (mpl)
museum	le musée
mushroom	le champignon
music	la musique
mussel	la moule
must	devoir
I must	je dois
mustard	la moutarde
mutton	le mouton

nail *(metal)*	le clou
(finger)	l'ongle *(m)*
nail polish	le vernis à ongles
nail polish remover	le dissolvant
name	le nom
napkin	la serviette de table
nappy	la couche
narrow	étroit(e)
nationality	la nationalité
navy blue	bleu marine
near	près
near the bank	*près de la banque*
necessary	nécessaire
neck	le cou
necklace	le collier
need	avoir besoin de
I need ...	*j'ai besoin de ...*
needle	l'aiguille *(f)*
negative *(photography)*	le négatif
neighbour	le/la voisin(e)
nephew	le neveu
nest	le nid
network	le réseau
never	jamais
I never drink wine	*je ne bois jamais de vin*
new	nouveau (nouvelle)
news	la nouvelle
newsagent	le marchand de journaux
newspaper	le journal
New Year	le Nouvel An
next: *the next train*	*le prochain train*
next week	*la semaine prochaine*
nice	bien ; bon (bonne) ; joli(e)
(person)	sympathique

niece	la nièce
night	la nuit
night club	la boîte de nuit
nightdress	la chemise de nuit
nightingale	le rossignol
no	non
no thank you	non merci
nobody	personne
noisy	bruyant(e)
non-alcoholic	non alcoolisé(e)
none	aucun(e)
non-smoking	non-fumeur
noodles	les nouilles (fpl)
north	le nord
Northern Ireland	l'Irlande (f) du Nord
nose	le nez
not	pas
I am not ...	je ne suis pas ...
note (banknote)	le billet
(letter)	la note
note pad	le bloc-notes
nothing	rien
notice	l'avis (m)
noun	le nom
novel	le roman
now	maintenant
number	le nombre ; le chiffre
(telephone)	le numéro
numberplate	la plaque (d'immatriculation)
numerous	nombreux (-euse)
nurse	l'infirmier/l'infirmière (m/f)
nursery slope	la piste pour débutants
nut (to eat)	la noix
(for bolt)	l'écrou (m)

oak	le chêne
oar	l'aviron (m); la rame
oats	l'avoine (f)
object	l'objet (m); la chose
obtain	obtenir
obvious	évident(e)
occasionally	de temps en temps
occupation (work)	l'emploi (m)
odd (number)	impair(e)
of	de
off (light)	éteint(e)
(rotten)	mauvais(e) ; pourri(e)
offer	offrir
office	le bureau
often	souvent
oil	l'huile (f)
oil filter	le filtre à huile
ointment	la pommade
OK	bien
old	vieux (vieille)
how old are you?	quel âge avez-vous?
olive oil	l'huile (f) d'olive
olives	les olives (f)
omelette	l'omelette (f)
on (light)	allumé(e)
(engine, etc.)	en marche
on the table	sur la table
once	une fois
one	un/une
one-way (street)	à sens unique
onion	l'oignon (m)
only	seulement
open adj	ouvert(e)
open vb	ouvrir

opening	l'ouverture (f)
opera	l'opéra (m)
operator	le/la téléphoniste
opposite	en face de
optional	facultatif (-ive)
or	ou
orally (take medicine)	par voie orale
orange adj	orange
orange n	l'orange (f)
orange juice	le jus d'orange
orchard	le verger
order	commander
original	original(e)
other	autre
out (light)	éteint(e)
she's out	elle est sortie
outdoor (pool, etc.)	en plein air
outside	à l'extérieur
oven	le four
over (on top of)	au-dessus de
overbook	faire du surbooking
overcharge	faire payer trop cher
overdraft	le découvert
overheat	surchauffer
overload	surcharger
overnight (travel)	de nuit
overtake	doubler ; dépasser
owe	devoir
you owe me ...	vous me devez ...
owl	le hibou ; la chouette
own	posséder
owner	le/la propriétaire
oyster	l'huître (f)

pace	le pas
pack *(luggage)*	emballer
package	le paquet
package tour	le voyage organisé
packet	le paquet
page	la page
paid	payé(e)
painful	douloureux (-euse)
painkiller	le calmant
painting	le tableau
pair	la paire
palace	le palais
pan	la casserole
pancake	la crêpe
pants	le slip
paper	le papier
paraffin	le pétrole
paralysed	paralysé(e)
parcel	le colis
pardon?	comment?
I beg your pardon!	pardon!
parents	les parents *(mpl)*
Paris	Paris
park *n*	le parc
park *vb*	garer (la voiture)
parking disk	le disque de stationnement
parsley	le persil
part	la partie
partridge	la perdrix
party *(group)*	le groupe
(celebration)	la fête ; la soirée
passenger	le passager/la passagère
passport	le passeport
passport control	le contrôle des passeports

pasta	les pâtes *(fpl)*
pastry	la pâte
(cake)	la pâtisserie
pâté	le pâté
path	le chemin
pay	payer
payment	le paiement
peach	la pêche
peanut	la cacahuète
pear	la poire
peas	les petits pois
pebbles	les cailloux *(mpl)* ; les galets *(mpl)*
pedestrian	le/la piéton(ne)
peel *(fruit)*	peler
peg *(for clothes)*	la pince à linger
(for tent)	le piquet
pen	le stylo
pencil	le crayon
penicillin	la pénicilline
penknife	le canif
pensioner	le retraité/la retraitée
pepper *(spice)*	le poivre
(vegetable)	le poivron
per: *per hour*	à l'heure
perfect	parfait(e)
performance	la représentation
perfume	le parfum
perhaps	peut-être
period *(menstruation)*	les règles *(fpl)*
perm	la permanente
permit	le permis
person	la personne
petrol	l'essence *(f)*
petrol station	la station-service

petrol tank	le réservoir
pheasant	le faisan
phone	téléphoner
photocopy	photocopier
photograph	la photo
picnic	le pique-nique
picture *(painting)*	le tableau
(photo)	la photo
pie	la tourte
piece	le morceau
pig	le cochon
pill	la pilule
pillow	l'oreiller *(m)*
pillowcase	la taie d'oreiller
pin	l'épingle *(f)*
pineapple	l'ananas *(m)*
pink	rose
pint	= approx. 0.5 kilo
a pint of ...	un demi-litre de ...
pipe *(for water, gas)*	le tuyau
(smoking)	la pipe
plane	l'avion *(m)*
plaster *(sticking plaster)*	le sparadrap
plastic	le plastique
plate	l'assiette *(f)*
platform	le quai
play *(games)*	jouer
playroom	la salle de jeux
pleasant	agréable
please	s'il vous plaît
pleased	content(e)
pliers	la pince
plug *(electrical)*	la prise
plum	la prune

plumber	le plombier
points *(in car)*	les vis *(fpl)* platinées
police	la police
policeman	l'agent *(m)* de police
police station	le commissariat ; la gendarmerie
polish *(for shoes)*	le cirage
polluted	pollué(e)
pony-trekking	la randonnée à cheval
pool *(swimming)*	la piscine
poor	pauvre
popular	populaire
pork	le porc
port *(seaport)*	le port
(wine)	le porto
porter *(in hotel)*	le porteur
possible	possible
post *vb*	poster
postbox	la boîte aux lettres
postcard	la carte postale
postcode	le code postal
post office	la poste
pot *(for cooking)*	la casserole
potato	la pomme de terre
pottery	la poterie
pound *(money)*	la livre
pound *(weight)*	= *approx. 0.5 kilo*
powdered milk	le lait en poudre
practise	pratiquer
pram	le landau
prawn	la crevette
pray	prier
prefer	préférer
pregnant	enceinte

prepare	préparer
prescription	l'ordonnance (f)
present (gift)	le cadeau
pretty	joli(e)
price	le prix
price list	le tarif
priest	le prêtre
print n (photo)	l'épreuve (f)
print vb	imprimer
private	privé(e)
prize	le prix
probably	probablement
problem	le problème
programme	le programme
pronounce	prononcer
how's it pronounced?	comment ça se prononce?
Protestant	protestant(e)
provide	fournir
prune	le pruneau
public	public (-que)
public holiday	le jour férié
pudding	le dessert
pull	tirer
puncture	la crevaison
puppet	la marionnette
purple	violet (-ette)
purpose: on purpose	exprès
purse	le porte-monnaie
push	pousser
push chair	la poussette
put (insert)	mettre
(put down)	déposer
pyjamas	le pyjama
Pyrenees	les Pyrénées (fpl)

queen	la reine
question	la question
queue	la queue
quick	rapide
quickly	vite
quiet *(place)*	tranquille
quilt	la couette
quite *(rather)*	assez
(completely)	complètement

rabbit	le lapin
rabies	la rage
race *(people)*	la race
(sport)	la course
racket	la raquette
radio	la radio
radish	le radis
rag	le chiffon
railway	le chemin de fer
railway station	la gare
rain	la pluie
rainbow	l'arc-en-ciel *(m)*
raincoat	l'imperméable *(m)*
raining: *it's raining*	il pleut
raisin	le raisin sec
rake	le râteau
rape	le viol
rare *(unique)*	rare
(steak)	saignant(e)
rash *(skin)*	la rougeur
raspberries	les framboises *(fpl)*
rate	le taux
(exchange)	le taux de change

raw	cru(e)
razor	le rasoir
razor blades	les lames *(fpl)* de rasoir
reader	le lecteur/la lectrice
ready	prêt(e)
real	vrai(e)
receipt	le reçu
receiver *(telephone)*	le récepteur
recently	récemment
reception *(desk)*	la réception
recharge *(battery, etc.)*	recharger
recipe	la recette
recognize	reconnaître
recommend	recommander
record *(music, etc.)*	le disque
red	rouge
reduce	réduire
reduction	la réduction
reel *(fishing)*	le moulinet
referee	l'arbitre *(m)*
refill	la recharge
refund	le remboursement
registered	recommandé(e)
regulation	le règlement
rehearse	répéter
reimburse	rembourser
relation *(family)*	le parent
relationship	le rapport
relax	se détendre
reliable *(service)*	sérieux (-euse)
remain	rester
remember	se rappeler
remove	enlever

rent	louer
rental	la location
repair	réparer
repay	rembourser
repeat	répéter
request	la demande
require	avoir besoin de
reschedule	changer l'heure/la date de
rescue	sauver
reservation	la réservation
reserve	réserver
reserved	réservé(e)
resident	l'habitant(e) (m/f)
resort (seaside)	la station balnéaire
rest n (repose)	le repos
the rest of the wine	le reste du vin
rest vb	se reposer
restaurant	le restaurant
restaurant car	le wagon-restaurant
retail	la vente au détail
return (go back)	retourner
(give back)	rendre
return ticket	le billet aller et retour
reverse charge call	l'appel (m) en P.C.V.
rhubarb	la rhubarbe
rib	la côte
ribbon	le ruban
rice	le riz
rich	riche
riding	l'équitation (f)
(go riding)	faire du cheval/de l'équitation
right adj (correct)	exact(e)
right n	la droite
on/to the right	à droite

ring n	la bague
ring vb (bell)	sonner
riot	l'émeute (f)
ripe	mûr(e)
river	la rivière
Riviera (French)	la Côte d'Azur
road	la route
road map	la carte routière
road sign	le panneau
roast	rôti(e)
robin	le rouge-gorge
roll (bread)	le petit pain
roof	le toit
roof-rack	la galerie
room (in house, hotel)	la pièce
(space)	la place
room service	le service d'étage
rope	la corde
rough sea	la grosse mer
round	rond(e)
round the corner	en tournant le coin
roundabout	le rond-point
route	la route ; l'itinéraire (m)
rowing boat	le bateau à rames
rubber	le caoutchouc
rubber band	l'élastique (m)
rubbish	les ordures (fpl)
rucksack	le sac à dos
ruins	les ruines (f)
rum	le rhum
run n (ski)	la piste
run vb	courir
runway (airport)	la piste
rush hour	l'heure (f) de pointe

sack	le sac
sad	triste
saddle	la selle
safe *n*	le coffre-fort
safe *adj*	sans danger ; en sûreté
safety pin	l'épingle (f) de sûreté
sage *(herb)*	la sauge
sail	la voile
sailboard	la planche à voile
sailing *(sport)*	la voile
salad	la salade
salad dressing	la vinaigrette
salary	le salaire
sale	la vente ; les soldes (fpl)
salesman/woman	le vendeur/la vendeuse
salmon	le saumon
salt	le sel
same	même
sample	l'échantillon (m)
sand	le sable
sandals	les sandales (fpl)
sandwich	le sandwich
sandy *(beach)*	de sable
sanitary towel	la serviette hygiénique
sardine	la sardine
Saturday	(le) samedi
sauce	la sauce
saucepan	la casserole
saucer	la soucoupe
sauna	le sauna
sausage	la saucisse
save *(life)*	sauver
(money)	épargner

savoury (not sweet)	salé(e)
saw n	la scie
say	dire
scales (for weighing)	la balance
scallop	la coquille Saint-Jacques
scarecrow	l'épouvantail (m)
scarf	l'écharpe (f)
scene (theatre)	la scène
scenery	le paysage
scent	le parfum
schedule	le programme
school	l'école (f)
scissors	les ciseaux (mpl)
score (goal, point)	marquer
Scotland	l'Écosse (f)
Scottish	écossais(e)
scrape	gratter
screen (computer, TV)	l'écran (m)
screw	la vis
screwdriver	le tournevis
sculpture (object)	la sculpture
sea	la mer
seafood	les fruits (mpl) de mer
seagull	la mouette
seal (animal)	le phoque
seam (of garment)	la couture
seasickness	le mal de mer
seaside: at the seaside	au bord de la mer
season ticket	l'abonnement (m)
seat (chair)	le siège
(in train, theatre)	la place
second	deuxième
second class	en deuxième

secondhand	d'occasion
secretary	la secrétaire
section	la partie
sedative	le calmant
see	voir
seed	la semence ; la graine
seize	saisir
self-employed (to be)	travailler à son compte
selfish	égoïste
self-service	le libre-service
sell	vendre
Sellotape®	le Scotch®
send	envoyer
senior citizen	la personne du troisième âge
sensible	raisonnable
sentence	la phrase
separate	séparé(e)
sequel (book, film)	la suite
serious	grave
serve	servir
service (in restaurant)	le service
service charge	le service
set menu	le menu
settee	le canapé
settle	régler
several	plusieurs
sew	coudre
sex	le sexe
shade	l'ombre (f)
shadow	l'ombre (f)
shake (bottle, etc.)	agiter
shallow	peu profond(e)
shampoo	le shampooing

shampoo and set	le shampooing et mise en plis
shandy	le panaché
shape	la forme
share	partager
shares *(stocks)*	les actions *(fpl)*
shave	se raser
shaving cream	la crème à raser
she	elle *see* GRAMMAR
sheet	le drap
shelf	le rayon ; l'étagère *(f)*
shell	la coquille
shellfish	le crustacé
sheltered	abrité(e)
shepherd	le berger
sherry	le sherry
shine	briller
ship	le navire
shirt	la chemise
shock absorber	l'amortisseur *(m)*
shoe	la chaussure
shoelaces	les lacets *(mpl)*
shop	le magasin
shopping *(to go)*	faire des courses
shore	le rivage
short	court(e)
shortage	le manque
short cut	le raccourci
shortly	bientôt
shorts	le short
shoulder	l'épaule *(f)*
shout	crier
show *n*	le spectacle
show *vb*	montrer

shower	la douche
shrimp	la crevette grise
shrink *(clothes)*	rétrécir
shut *adj*	fermé(e)
shut *vb*	fermer
shutter *(on window)*	le volet
shy	timide
sick *(ill)*	malade
sightseeing	le tourisme
sign	le panneau
signature	la signature
silk	la soie
silver	l'argent *(m)*
similar (to)	semblable (à)
simple	simple
since	depuis
single *(unmarried)*	célibataire
(not double)	simple
(bed, room)	pour une personne
sink	l'évier *(m)*
sir	Monsieur
sister	la sœur
sit	s'asseoir
sit down	asseyez-vous
size *(clothes)*	la taille
(shoe)	la pointure
skate	le patin
skating *(ice)*	le patinage sur glace
(roller)	le skating ; le patinage à roulettes
ski *vb*	faire du ski
ski *n*	le ski
ski boots	les chaussures *(fpl)* de ski
skiing	le ski
skilled	adroit(e) ; qualifié(e)

skimmed milk	le lait écrémé
skin	la peau
skin diving	la plongée sous-marine
ski pants	le fuseau
ski pass	le forfait
ski pole	le bâton (de ski)
skirt	la jupe
ski run	la piste
ski suit	la combinaison de ski
sky	le ciel
slang	l'argot (m)
slate	l'ardoise (f)
sledge	la luge
sleep	dormir
sleeping bag	le sac de couchage
sleeping car	la voiture-lit
sleep in	dormir tard
sleeping pill	le somnifère
sleeve	la manche
slice	la tranche
sliced bread	le pain en tranches
slide (photograph)	la diapositive
slip	glisser
slippers	les pantoufles (fpl)
slope	la pente
slot	la fente
slow	lent(e)
slow down	ralentir
small	petit(e)
smaller than	plus petit(e) que
smell	l'odeur (f)
smile vb	sourire
smoke n	la fumée

smoke vb	fumer
smoked	fumé(e)
smooth	lisse
snack	le casse-croûte
snack bar	le snack-bar
snail	l'escargot (m)
snake	le serpent
sneeze	éternuer
snorkel	le tuba
snow	la neige
snowed up	enneigé(e)
snowing: it's snowing	il neige
so: so much	tant
soap	le savon
soap powder	la lessive
sock	la chaussette
socket	la prise de courant
soda	l'eau (f) gazeuse
soft	doux (douce)
soft drink	la boisson non alcoolisée
soil	la terre
some	quelques
someone	quelqu'un
something	quelque chose
sometimes	quelquefois
son	le fils
song	la chanson
soon	bientôt
sore	douloureux (-euse)
sorry: I'm sorry!	excusez-moi!
sort	la sorte ; le genre
sound	le bruit
soup	le potage ; la soupe

sour	aigre
south	le sud
souvenir	le souvenir
spa	la station thermale
space	la place
spade	la pelle
Spain	l'Espagne (f)
Spanish	espagnol(e)
spanner	la clé
spare tyre	le pneu de rechange
spare wheel	la roue de rechange
sparkling (wine)	mousseux (-euse)
spark plug	la bougie
sparrow	le moineau
speak	parler
special	spécial(e)
speciality	la spécialité
speed	la vitesse
speed limit	la limitation de vitesse
spell: how is it spelt?	comment ça s'écrit?
spice	l'épice (f)
spicy	épicé(e)
spider	l'araignée (f)
spinach	les épinards (mpl)
spin dryer	l'essoreuse (f)
spirits	les spiritueux (mpl)
splinter (in finger)	l'écharole (f)
sponge	l'éponge (f)
spoon	la cuiller
sport	le sport
sprain	l'entorse (f)
spring (season)	le printemps
square (in town)	la place

squash (game)	le squash
(drink)	la citronnade/l'orangeade (f)
squeeze	presser
stage	la scène
stain	la tache
stairs	l'escalier (m)
stalls (theatre)	l'orchestre (m)
stamp	le timbre
start	commencer
starter (in meal)	le hors d'oeuvre
(in car)	le démarreur
station	la gare
stationer's	la papeterie
stay (remain)	rester
I'm staying at ..	je suis à ...
steak	le bifteck
steal	voler
steel	l'acier (m)
steep	raide
step	le pas
sterling	le sterling
stew	le ragoût
steward	le steward
stewardess	l'hôtesse (f)
sticking plaster	le sparadrap
still (motionless)	immobile
sting	la piqûre
stockings	les bas (mpl)
stomach	l'estomac (m)
stomach upset	l'estomac (m) dérangé
stone	la pierre
stop	arrêter
stopover	la halte
storey	l'étage (m)

storm	l'orage *(m)*
story	l'histoire *(f)*
straight on	tout droit
straw *(for drinking)*	la paille
strawberry	la fraise
stream	le ruisseau
street	la rue
street map	le plan des rues
strength	la force
stress	la pression
strike	la grève
string	la ficelle
striped	rayé(e)
stroll *(to go for)*	aller faire un tour
strong	fort(e)
stuck	bloqué(e)
student *(male)*	l'étudiant
(female)	l'étudiante
stuff	la chose
stung	piqué(e)
stupid	stupide
succeed	réussir à
suddenly	soudain
suede	le daim
sugar	le sucre
suit *(man's)*	le costume
(women's)	le tailleur
suitcase	la valise
sum	la somme
summer	l'été *(m)*
sun	le soleil
sunbathe	prendre un bain de soleil
sunburn	le coup de soleil

sunglasses	les lunettes *(fpl)* de soleil
sunny: it's sunny	il fait du soleil
sunscreen *(lotion)*	l'écran *(m)* solaire
sunshade	le parasol
sunstroke	l'insolation *(f)*
suntan lotion	le lait solaire
supermarket	le supermarché
supper *(dinner)*	le souper
supplement	le supplément
supply	fournir
sure	sûr(e)
surfboard	la planche de surf
surfing	le surf
surname	le nom de famille
surprise	la surprise
swallow *n (bird)*	l'hirondelle *(f)*
swallow *vb*	avaler
swan	le cygne
sweater	le pull
sweet	sucré(e)
sweetener	l'édulcorant *(m)*
sweets	les bonbons *(mpl)*
swim	nager
swimming pool	la piscine
swimsuit	le maillot de bain
swing	la balançoire
Swiss	suisse
switch	le bouton
switch off	éteindre
switch on	allumer
Switzerland	la Suisse
swollen	enflé(e)
synagogue	la synagogue

table	la table
tablecloth	la nappe
tablespoon	la cuiller de service
tablet	le comprimé
table tennis	le ping-pong
take	prendre
how long does it take?	*ça prend combien de temps?*
talc	le talc
talk	parler
tall	grand(e)
tampons	les tampons *(mpl)*
tan	le bronzage
tank	le réservoir
tap	le robinet
tape	le ruban
(cassette)	la cassette
tape-recorder	le magnétophone
tartar sauce	la sauce tartare
taste *vb*	goûter
taste *n*	le goût
tax	l'impôt *(m)*
taxi	le taxi
taxi rank	la station de taxis
tea	le thé
tea bag	le sachet de thé
teach	enseigner
teacher	le professeur
teapot	la théière
teaspoon	la cuiller à café
teeth	les dents *(mpl)*
telegram	le télégramme
telephone	le téléphone
telephone box	la cabine téléphonique
telephone call	le coup de téléphone

telephone directory	l'annuaire *(m)*
television	la télévision
telex	le télex
tell	dire
temperature	la température
(to have a temperature)	avoir de la fièvre
temporary	provisoire
tennis	le tennis
tennis court	le court de tennis
tennis racket	la raquette de tennis
tent	la tente
tent peg	le piquet de tente
terminal *(airport)*	l'aérogare *(f)*
terrace	la terrasse
than	que
thank you	merci
thank you very much	*merci beaucoup*
that	cela
that one	*celui-là*
thaw: *it's thawing*	il dégèle
theatre	le théâtre
then	alors
there	là
there is/are...	*il y a...*
thermometer	le thermomètre
these	ceux-ci
they	ils/elles *see* GRAMMAR
thief	le voleur/la voleuse
thing	la chose
my things	*mes affaires*
think	penser
thirsty: *I'm thirsty*	j'ai soif
this	ceci
this one	*celui-ci*

thorn	l'épine (f)
those	ceux-là
thread	le fil
throat	la gorge
throat lozenges	les pastilles (fpl) pour la gorge
through	à travers
thunderstorm	l'orage (m)
ticket	le billet
ticket collector	le contrôleur
ticket office	le guichet
tide	la marée
tie	la cravate
tight (fitting)	serré(e)
tights	le collant
till n	la caisse
till prep	jusqu'à
time	le temps
this time	cette fois
timetable	l'horaire (m)
(in school)	l'emploi (m) du temps
tin	la boîte
tinfoil	le papier d'alu(minium)
tin-opener	l'ouvre-boîtes (m)
tip (to waiter, etc.)	le pourboire
tipped (cigarette)	à bout filtre
tired	fatigué(e)
tissue	le kleenex®
to	à
(with name of country)	en
toad	le crapaud
toast	le toast
tobacconist's	le bureau de tabac
today	aujourd'hui
together	ensemble

toilet	les toilettes *(fpl)*
toilet paper	le papier hygiénique
toll	le péage
tomato	la tomate
tomorrow	demain
tongue	la langue
tonic water	le Schweppes®
tonight	ce soir
too *(also)*	aussi
it's too big	*c'est trop grand*
tooth	la dent
toothbrush	la brosse à dents
toothpaste	le dentifrice
top *adj : the top floor*	*le dernier étage*
top *n*	le dessus
on top of	*sur*
torch	la lampe de poche
torn	déchiré(e)
tough *(meat)*	dur(e)
tour	l'excursion *(f)*
tourist	le/la touriste
tourist office	le syndicat d'initiative
tourist ticket	le billet touristique
tow	remorquer
towel	la serviette
town	la ville
town centre	le centre ville
town plan	le plan de la ville
tow rope	le câble de remorque
toy	le jouet
traditional	traditionnel (-elle)
traffic	la circulation
trailer	la remorque
train	le train

training shoes	les chaussures *(fpl)* de sport
tram	le tramway
translate	traduire
translation	la traduction
travel	voyager
travel agent	l'agent *(m)* de voyages
traveller's cheque	le chèque de voyage
tray	le plateau
tree	l'arbre *(m)*
trip	l'excursion *(f)*
trouble	les ennuis *(mpl)*
trousers	le pantalon
true	vrai(e)
trunk *(luggage)*	la malle
trunks	le slip (de bain)
try	essayer
try on *(clothes)*	essayer
tuna	le thon
tunnel	le tunnel
turkey	la dinde
turn *(handle, wheel)*	tourner
turnip	le navet
turn off *(light, etc)*	éteindre
(engine)	arrêter le moteur
turn on *(light, etc.)*	allumer
(engine)	mettre en marche
tweezers	la pince à épiler
twice	deux fois
twin-bedded room	la chambre à deux lits
twinned with *(town)*	jumelé(e) avec
typical	typique
tyre	le pneu
tyre pressure	la pression des pneus

ugly	laid(e)
umbrella	le parapluie
umpire	l'arbitre (m)
uncle	l'oncle (m)
uncomfortable	inconfortable
uncommon	rare
unconscious	sans connaissance
under	sous
undercooked	pas assez cuit(e)
underground	le métro
underpants (man's)	le caleçon
underpass	le passage souterrain
understand	comprendre
I don't understand	*je ne comprends pas*
underwear	les sous-vêtements (mpl)
unemployed	au chômage
United Kingdom	le Royaume-Uni
United States	les États Unis (mpl)
university	l'université (f)
unkind	pas gentil (-ille)
unleaded petrol	l'essence (f) sans plomb
unload	décharger
unpack (case)	défaire
unpleasant	désagréable
unskilled	non qualifié(e)
unwell	malade
up (out of bed)	levé(e)
up there	*là-haut*
upstairs	en haut
urgent	urgent(e)
use	utiliser
useful	utile
usual	habituel (-elle)
usually	habituellement

vacancy *(in hotel)*	la chambre à louer
vacuum cleaner	l'aspirateur *(m)*
valid	valable
valley	la vallée
valuable	d'une grande valeur
valuables	les objets *(mpl)* de valeur
value	la valeur
valve	la valve
van	la camionnette
variety	la variété
vase	le vase
VAT	la TVA
veal	le veau
vegetables	les légumes *(mpl)*
vegetarian	végétarien(ne)
velvet	le velours
ventilator	le ventilateur
vermouth	le vermouth
very	très
vest	le maillot de corps
via	par
video *(recorder)*	le magnétoscope
view	la vue
villa	la maison de campagne
village	le village
vinegar	le vinaigre
vineyard	le vignoble
visa	le visa
visit	visiter
vitamin	la vitamine
voice	la voix
vodka	la vodka
voltage	le voltage

wage	le salaire
waist	la taille
wait (for)	attendre
waiter	le garçon
waiting room	la salle d'attente
waitress	la serveuse
wake up	se réveiller
Wales	le pays de Galles
walk *vb*	aller à pied ; marcher
walk : to go for a walk	*faire une promenade*
wall	le mur
wallet	le portefeuille
walnut	la noix
want	désirer ; vouloir
war	la guerre
warm	chaud(e)
warm up *(milk, etc.)*	chauffer ; faire chauffer
warning triangle	le triangle de présignalisation
wash	laver
(to wash oneself)	se laver
washbasin	le lavabo
washing machine	la machine à laver
washing powder	la lessive
washing-up liquid	le lave-vaisselle
wasp	la guêpe
waste bin	la poubelle
watch *n*	la montre
watch *vb (look at)*	regarder
water	l'eau *(f)*
waterfall	les chutes *(fpl)* d'eau ; la cascade
water heater	le chauffe-eau
watermelon	la pastèque
waterproof	imperméable

water-skiing	le ski nautique
wave (on sea)	la vague
wax	la cire
way (manner)	la manière
(route)	le chemin
we	nous *see* **GRAMMAR**
weak	faible
(coffee, etc.)	léger (-ère)
wear	porter
weather	le temps
web (spider)	la toile
wedding	le mariage
week	la semaine
weekday	le jour de semaine
weekend	le weekend
weekly	par semaine ; hebdomadaire
weigh	peser
weight	le poids
welcome	bienvenu(e)
well n (water)	le puits
(fit)	en bonne santé
well done (steak)	bien cuit(e)
Welsh	gallois(e)
west	l'ouest (m)
wet	mouillé(e)
wetsuit	la combinaison de plongée
what	que ; quel/quelle ; quoi
what is it?	*qu'est-ce que c'est?*
wheel	la roue
wheelchair	le fauteuil roulant
when	quand
where	où
which	quel/quelle
which is it?	*c'est lequel/laquelle?*

while	pendant que
whipped cream	la crème fouettée
whisky	le whisky
white	blanc (blanche)
who	qui
whole	entier
wholemeal bread	le pain complet
whose: whose is it?	c'est à qui?
why	pourquoi
wide	large
widow	la veuve
widower	le veuf
width	la largeur
wife	la femme
win	gagner
windmill	le moulin à vent
window	la fenêtre
(shop)	la vitrine
windscreen	le pare-brise
windsurfing	la planche à voile
wine	le vin
wine list	la carte des vins
wing (bird, aircraft)	l'aile (f)
winter	l'hiver (m)
with	avec
without	sans
woman	la femme
wonderful	merveilleux (-euse)
wood	le bois
wool	la laine
word	le mot
work vb (person)	travailler
(machine, car)	fonctionner ; marcher
world	le monde

worried	inquiet (-iète)
worse	pire
worth: *it's worth ...*	*ça vaut ...*
wrap (up)	envelopper
wrapping paper	le papier d'emballage
wrinkles	les rides *(fpl)*
wrist	le poignet
write	écrire
writing paper	le papier à lettres
wrong	faux (fausse) ; incorrect(e)
X-ray	la radiographie
yacht	le yacht
year	l'an *(m)*
yearly	annuellement
yellow	jaune
yes	oui
yes please	*oui merci*
yesterday	hier
yet: *not yet*	*pas encore*
you	vous
(with friends)	tu see **GRAMMAR**
young	jeune
youth hostel	l'auberge *(f)* de jeunesse
zebra crossing	le passage pour piétons
zero	le zéro
zip	la fermeture éclair
zone	la zone
zoo	le zoo

à	to ; at
abats *mpl*	offal ; giblets
abbaye *f*	abbey
abonné(e) *m/f*	subscriber ; season ticket holder
abonnement *m*	subscription ; season ticket
abri *m*	shelter
abricot *m*	apricot
accès *m*	access
accès interdit	no entry
accès réservé	authorized entrance only
accès aux quais	to the trains
accident *m*	accident
accompagné(e)	accompanied
accotement *m*	verge
accueil *m*	reception
accueillir	to greet ; to welcome
A.C.F. *m*	Automobile Club de France
achat *m*	purchase
acheter	to buy
acier *m*	steel
activité *f*	activity
addition *f*	bill
adhérent(e) *m/f*	member
adresser	to address
adressez-vous à	enquire at *(office)*
aérogare *f*	terminal
aéroglisseur *m*	hovercraft
aéroport *m*	airport
affaires *fpl*	business ; belongings
bonnes affaires	bargains
affiche *f*	poster ; notice
afin de	in order to
âgé(e)	elderly
âgé de	aged

agence f	agency ; branch
agence immobilière	estate agency
agence de voyages	travel agency
agenda m	diary
agent m	agent
agent de police	policeman
agiter	to shake (on bottle)
agiter avant emploi	shake before use
agneau m	lamb
agrandissement m	enlargement
agréable	pleasant ; nice
agréé(e)	registered ; authorized
aider	to help
aiglefin m	haddock
aigre	sour
à l'aigre-doux	sweet and sour
aiguille f	needle
ail m	garlic
aile f	wing
aïoli m	garlic mayonnaise
air: en plein air	(in the) open air
de plein air	outdoors
aire f : aire de jeux	play area
aire de repos	rest area
aire de services	service area
airelles fpl	bilberries ; cranberries
alcool m	alcohol ; fruit brandy
alcool à brûler	methylated spirits
alcoolisé(e)	alcoholic
alentours mpl	surrounding area ; outskirts
algues fpl	seaweed
alimentation f	food ; grocery shop
allée f	driveway ; path
Allemagne f	Germany
allemand(e)	German

aller	to go
aller-retour m	return ticket
aller (simple) m	single ticket
allumer	to turn on ; to light
allumez vos phares	switch on headlights
allumette f	match
alpinisme m	mountaineering ; climbing
alsacien(ne)	Alsatian
amande f	almond
pâte d'amandes	almond paste ; marzipan
ambassade f	embassy
améliorer	to improve
aménagements mpl	work(s) ; fittings
amende f	fine
amer (-ère)	bitter
ameublé(e)	furnished
ami(e) m/f	friend
an m	year
ananas m	pineapple
anchois m	anchovy
ancien(ne)	old ; former
à l'ancienne	in a wine, cream, mushroom sauce
andouille f	sausage made of chitterlings
andouillette f	small chitterling sausage
anglais(e)	English
Angleterre f	England
anguille f	eel
animation f	entertainment ; activity
animaux mpl	animals
anis m	aniseed
anisette f	aniseed liqueur
année f	year ; vintage
anniversaire m	anniversary ; birthday
annonce f	advertisement

annuaire m	directory
annulation f	cancellation
annuler	to cancel
antenne f	aerial
antiquaire m/f	antique dealer
A.O.C.	abbrev. of appellation d'origine contrôlée
août m	August
appareil m	appliance ; camera
appareil-photo m	camera
appartement m	apartment ; flat
appel m	call
appellation d'origine contrôlée	guarantee of quality and origin of a wine
appuyer	to push ; to press
après	after
après-midi m	afternoon
après-rasage m	after-shave
arachide f	groundnut
arbre m	tree
argent m	money ; silver (metal)
Armagnac m	brandy from Armagnac
arrêt m	stop ; off (machine)
arrêt d'autobus	bus stop
arrêt facultatif	request stop
arrêtez	stop
arrhes fpl	deposit (part payment)
arrière m	rear ; back
arrivées fpl	arrivals
arrondissement m	district (in Paris)
artichaut m	artichoke
fond d'artichaut	artichoke heart
article m	item ; article
artisan m	craftsman

artisanat m	arts and crafts
ascenseur m	lift
asperge f	asparagus
assaisonnement m	seasoning ; dressing
assiette f	plate
assiette anglaise	assorted cold meats
assiette de crudités	selection of raw vegetables
assorti(e)	assorted ; matching
assortiment m	assortment
assurance f	insurance
assuré(e)	insured
parking assuré	parking facilities
assurer	to assure ; to insure
atelier m	workshop ; artist's studio
attacher	to fasten
attendre	to wait (for) ; wait!
attention	look out!
attention au feu	danger of fire
attestation f	certificate
attirer l'attention	to bring to attention
auberge f	inn
auberge de jeunesse	youth hostel
aubergine f	aubergine
aucun(e)	none ; no ; not any
au-delà de	beyond
au gratin	baked with cheese topping
aujourd'hui	today
au revoir	goodbye
aussi	also
autobus m	bus
autocar m	coach
auto-école f	driving school
automne m	autumn
automobiliste m/f	motorist

autorisé(e)	permitted ; authorized
autoroute f	motorway
auto-stop m	hitchhiking
autre	other
autres directions	other routes
avaler	to swallow
ne pas avaler	not to be taken internally
avance f	advance
à l'avance	in advance
d'avance	in advance
avant	before ; front
à l'avant	at the front
avec	with
avertir	to inform ; to warn
aveugle	blind
avion m	plane
aviron m	oar ; rowing (sport)
avis m	notice ; warning
avocat m	avocado ; lawyer
avoine f	oats
avoir	to have
avril m	April
baba au rhum m	rum baba
bagages mpl	luggage
baguette f	stick of (French) bread
baignade f	bathing
bain m	bath
bal m	ball ; dance
balcon m	circle (in theatre) ; balcony
ballon m	balloon ; ball ; brandy glass
ball-trap m	clay pigeon shooting
banane f	banana

banc m	seat ; bench
banlieue f	suburbs
de banlieue	suburban
banque f	bank
bar m	bar
bar à café	unlicensed bar (Switz.)
bar m	bass (fish)
barbue f	brill
barquette f	punnet ; small tart
barrage m	dam
barrage routier	road block
barré: route barrée	road closed
barrer	to cross out
barrière f	barrier
Barsac m	sweet white wine from Bordeaux
bas m	bottom (of page, list, etc.) ; stocking
en bas	below ; downstairs
bas(se)	low
basilic m	basil
bassin m	pond
batavia f	Webb lettuce
bateau m	boat ; ship
bateau-mouche	river boat ; pleasure steamer
bâtiment m	building
bavaroise f	mousse of egg yolk and cream
bavette (échalotes) f	type of steak with shallots
béarnaise	classic rich creamy sauce
beau	lovely ; fine
beaucoup (de)	much ; many ; a lot of
Beaujolais m	light, fruity wine drunk young
bébé m	baby
bécasse f	woodcock
bécassine f	snipe
béchamel f	white sauce

beignet *m*	fritter ; doughnut
Belgique *f*	Belgium
belle	lovely
Bénédictine *f*	greenish-yellow liqueur
Bercy *f*	white wine and shallot sauce
berlingots *mpl*	boiled sweets
besoin : avoir besoin	to need ; to require
betterave *f*	beetroot
beurre *m*	butter
beurre d'anchois	anchovy paste
beurre doux	unsalted butter
bibliothèque *f*	library
bien	well ; right ; good
bientôt	soon ; shortly
bière *f*	beer
bière blonde	lager
bière brune	bitter
bière à la pression	draught beer
bifteck *m*	steak
bigarade *f*	orange sauce served with duck
bijoux *mpl*	jewellery
bijouterie *f*	jeweller's ; jewellery
billet *m*	ticket ; note
billet aller-retour	return ticket
billet de banque	banknote
billet simple	one-way ticket
biscotte *f*	breakfast biscuit ; rusk
biscuit *m*	biscuit
biscuit de Savoie	sponge cake
bisque *f*	thick seafood soup
blanc	white ; blank
blanc (de poulet)	breast of chicken
laissez en blanc	leave blank *(on form)*
blanche	white ; blank
blanchisserie *f*	laundry

blanquette *f*	casserole with cream sauce
blé *m*	wheat
bleu(e)	blue ; very rare *(steak)*
bleu d'Auvergne	sharp and salty rich blue cheese
bleu de bresse	mild soft blue cheese
bleu marine	navy blue
blonde	light *(beer)*
bloquer	to block
boeuf *m*	beef
boeuf bourguignon	beef stew in red wine
boeuf en daube	beef casserole
boeuf miroton	boiled beef in onion sauce
boire	to drink
bois *m*	wood
boisson *f*	drink
boîte *f*	can ; box
boîte aux lettres	letter box
boîte de nuit	night club
bolet *m*	boletus mushroom
bombe *f*	aerosol
bombe glacée	ice cream dessert
bon *m*	token ; voucher
bon(ne)	good ; right
bon marché	cheap
bonbons *mpl*	sweets
bonjour	hello ; good morning/afternoon
bonne	see bon(ne)
bonneterie *f*	hosiery
bonsoir	good evening
bord *m*	border ; edge ; verge
à bord	on board
le bord de (la) mer	seaside
Bordeaux *m*	claret
bordelaise, à la	cooked in wine and shallots
botte *f*	boot ; bunch

bouche d'incendie f	fire hydrant
bouchée f	chocolate
bouchée à la reine	chicken vol-au-vent
boucherie f	butcher's shop
boucle d'oreille f	earring
boudin m	black pudding
boudin blanc	white pudding
boue f	mud
bouillabaisse f	rich fish soup or stew
bouillir	to boil
bouillon m	stock
boulangerie f	bakery
boule f	ball
boules	game similar to bowls
Bourgogne f	Burgundy
bourguignonne, à la	cooked in red wine, onions, herbs
bourse f	stock exchange
bout m	end
bouteille f	bottle
boutique f	shop
bouton m	button ; switch
boxe f	boxing
braisé(e)	braised
brasserie f	café ; brewery
Bretagne f	Brittany
breton(ne)	from Brittany
bricolage m	do-it-yourself
brie m	soft, mild cow's-milk cheese
brioche f	brioche
briser	to break ; to smash
brocante f	second-hand goods ; flea market
broche f	brooch ; spit
à la broche	spit-roasted
brochet m	pike

brochette f	skewer ; kebab
brodé main	hand-embroidered
bronzage m	suntan
brouillard m	fog
brugnon m	nectarine
bruit m	noise
brûlé(e)	burnt
brun(e)	brown ; dark
brushing m	blow-dry
brut(e)	gross ; raw
(Champagne) brut	very dry Champagne
Bruxelles	Brussels
bulletin de consigne m	left-luggage ticket
bureau m	desk ; office
bureau de change	(foreign) exchange office
bureau de poste	post office
cabillaud m	(fresh) cod
cabine f	cabin ; cubicle
cabine d'essayage	changing room
cabinet m	office
cacahuète f	peanut
cacao m	cocoa
cadeau m	gift
café m	coffee ; café
café crème	white coffee
café décaféiné	decaffeinated coffee
café au lait	white coffee
café noir	black coffee
cafetière f	coffee pot
caille f	quail
caisse f	checkout ; cash desk ; case
caisse d'épargne	savings bank
caissier(ière) m/f	cashier ; teller

calendrier *m*	calendar ; timetable
calmar *m*	squid
calvados *m*	apple brandy
camembert *m*	soft, creamy cheese
camomille *f*	camomile
campagne *f*	country ; countryside ; campaign
camping *m*	camping ; camp-site
camping sauvage	camping on unofficial sites
camping-gaz *m*	camping stove
canapé *m*	sofa ; open sandwich
canard *m*	duck
canard à l'orange	duck in orange sauce
cannelle *f*	cinnamon
canot *m*	boat
canot de sauvetage	lifeboat
canotage *m*	boating
cantal *m*	hard cheese from the Auvergne
canton *m*	state *(Switz.)*
câpres *fpl*	capers
car *m*	coach
carafe *f*	carafe ; decanter
carnet *m*	notebook ; book
carotte *f*	carrot
carottes râpées	grated carrot in vinaigrette
carpe *f*	carp
carré *m*	square
carré de l'est	strong soft cheese
carrefour *m*	intersection ; crossroads
carrelet *m*	plaice
carte *f*	map ; card ; menu
carte d'abonnement	season ticket
carte bleue	credit card
carte du jour	menu of the day
carte orange	monthly or yearly season ticket
carte postale	postcard

carte vermeille	senior citizen's rail pass
carte des vins	wine list
cartouche f	carton (of cigarettes)
cas m	case
en cas de	in case of
cascade f	waterfall
case postale f	P.O. Box (Switz.)
caserne f	barracks
casier m	rack ; locker
casque m	helmet
casque à écouteurs	headphones
casse-croûte m	snack
cassis m	blackcurrant
crème de cassis	blackcurrant liqueur
cassolette f	individual fondue dish
cassonade f	brown sugar
cassoulet m	bean and pork stew
catch m	wrestling
cause f	cause
pour cause de	on account of
caution f	security (for loan) ; deposit
caution à verser	deposit required
cave f	cellar
caveau m	cellar
caviar m	caviar(e)
céder	to give in
cédez la priorité	give way (to traffic)
cédratine f	citron-based liqueur
CEE f	EC
ceinture f	belt
céleri m	celeriac ; celery
céleri rémoulade	celeriac in dressing
céleri-rave m	celeriac
célibataire	single
cendre f	ash

cendrier *m*	ashtray
cent	hundred
centre *m*	centre
centre commercial	shopping centre
centre équestre	riding school
centre ville	city centre
cèpes *mpl*	boletus mushrooms
cercle *m*	circle ; ring
cerfeuil *m*	chervil
cerise *f*	cherry
cervelle *f*	**brains** (as food)
cesser	to stop
cette	this ; that
ceux	the ones
ceux-ci	these
ceux-là	those
C.F.F. *mpl*	Swiss Railways
chaîne *f*	chain ; channel ; (mountain) range
chaînes obligatoires	snow chains compulsory
chaise *f*	chair
chaise haute	highchair
chalet *m*	chalet
Chambertin *m*	full-bodied red wine
chambre *f*	bedroom ; room
chambre à coucher	bedroom
chambre individuelle	single room
champ *m*	field
champ de courses	racecourse
champignon *m*	mushroom
champignon de Paris	button mushroom
change *m*	exchange
changement *m*	change
changer	to alter
changer de	to change
chanson *f*	song

chanterelle f	chanterelle (mushroom)
chantier m	building site ; roadworks
Chantilly	whipped cream
chapelle f	chapel
chaque	each ; every
charcuterie f	pork butcher's shop ; delicatessen
chariot m	trolley
charter m	charter flight
chartreuse f	liqueur made from herbs
chasse f	hunting ; shooting
chasse gardée	private hunting ; private shooting
chasse-neige m	snowplough
chasseur m	hunter
châtaigne f	chestnut
château m	castle ; mansion
chateaubriand m	thick fillet steak (usually for two)
chaud(e)	warm ; hot
chauffage m	heating
chauffeur m	chauffeur ; driver
chaussée f	carriageway
chaussée déformée	uneven road surface
chaussée rétrécie	road narrows
chaussée verglacée	icy/slippery road
chaussure f	shoe ; boot
chef m	chef ; chief ; head ; leader
chef-lieu m	county town
chemin m	path ; lane ; track
chemin de fer	railway
chemise f	shirt
chemisier m	blouse
chèque m	cheque
chèque de voyage	traveller's cheque
cher (chère)	dear ; expensive
cherry m	cherry brandy

cheval *m*	horse
cheveux *mpl*	hair
chèvre *f*	goat
chevreau *m*	kid *(leather)*
chevreuil *m*	roe deer ; venison
chez	at the house of
chicorée *f*	chicory *(for coffee)* ; endive
chien *m*	dog
chips *fpl*	crisps
chirurgien *m*	surgeon
chocolat *m*	chocolate ; drinking chocolate
chocolat à croquer	plain chocolate
chocolat au lait	milk chocolate
choix *m*	range ; choice ; selection
chope *f*	tankard
chou *m*	cabbage
chou à la crème	cream puff
choux de Bruxelles	Brussels sprouts
choucroute *f*	sauerkraut
chou-fleur *m*	cauliflower
chou-rave *m*	kohlrabi
C.H.U. *m*	hospital
chute *f*	fall
chutes (d'eau)	waterfall
ciboulette *f*	chives
cidre *m*	cider
ciel *m*	sky
cimetière *m*	cemetery ; graveyard
cintre *m*	coat hanger
cirage *m*	shoe polish
circuit *m*	(round) trip ; circuit
circulation *f*	traffic
cirque *m*	circus
cité *f*	city ; housing estate

citron *m*	lemon
citron pressé	fresh lemon drink
citron vert	lime
citronnade *f*	still lemonade
civet *m*	rich game stew
clair(e)	clear ; light
classe *f*	grade ; class
classe affaires	business class
clé *f*	key
clé de contact	ignition key
clé minute	keys cut while you wait
clef *f*	key
client(e) *m/f*	guest *(at hotel)* ; client ; customer
climatisé(e)	air-conditioned
clinique *f*	nursing home, (private) clinic
clou *m*	nail *(metal)*
clou de girofle	clove
cocher	to tick
cochon *m*	pig
cocotte *f*	casserole dish
cocotte-minute *f*	pressure cooker
cœur *m*	heart
coffre-fort *m*	strongbox ; safe
cognac *m*	brandy
coiffeur *m*	hairdresser ; barber
coiffeuse *f*	hairdresser ; dressing table
coin *m*	corner
Cointreau *m*	orange-based liqueur
col *m*	collar ; pass *(in mountains)*
colin *m*	hake
colis *m*	parcel
collant *m*	tights
collège *m*	secondary school
coller	to stick ; to glue

collier m	necklace ; dog collar
combien	how much/many
combustible m	fuel
commander	to order
commerçant(e) m/f	trader
commerce m	commerce ; business ; trade
commissariat m	police station
compagnie f	firm ; company
compartiment m	compartment *(train)*
complet (-ète)	full (up)
composer	to dial
composter	to date stamp/punch *(ticket)*
compote f	stewed fruit
comprenant	including
comprimé m	tablet
compris(e)	including
service compris	inclusive of service
tout compris	all inclusive
... non compris	exclusive of ...
comptant m	cash
compte m	account
compteur m	speedometer ; meter
comptoir m	bar
comté m	cheese similar to gruyère
concierge m/f	caretaker ; janitor
concombre m	cucumber
concours m	contest ; aid
conducteur (-trice) m/f	driver
conduite f	driving ; behaviour
confection f	ready-to-wear clothes
confiance f	confidence
de confiance	reliable
confirmer	to confirm
confiserie f	sweetshop

confit(e)	preserved
confiture f	jam ; preserve
confiture d'oranges	marmalade
congélateur m	freezer
congelé(e)	frozen
congre m	conger eel
conseil m	advice
conseil municipal	town council
conserver	to keep
consigne f	deposit ; left-luggage office
consommation f	consumption ; drink
consommé m	clear soup
constat m	report
contacter	to contact
contenu m	contents
contrat m	contract
contrat de location	lease
contre	against ; versus
contre-filet m	sirloin
contrôle m	check
contrôle radar	radar trap
contrôler	to check
contrôleur m	ticket inspector
convenu(e)	agreed
convoi m	load
coq m	cock(erel)
coque f	shell ; cockle
à la coque	soft boiled *(egg)*
coquet(te)	pretty *(place, etc.)*
coquillages mpl	shellfish
coquille f	shell
coquille Saint-Jacques	scallop
coquillettes fpl	pasta shells
corail m	coral ; type of train

cordonnerie *f*	cobbler's ; shoe repairing
cornet *m*	cone
corniche *f*	coast road
cornichon *m*	gherkin
corps *m*	body
correspondance *f*	connection *(train, plane)*
Corse *f*	Corsica
côte *f*	coast ; hill ; rib
côté *m*	side
à côté de	beside ; next to
Côte d'Azur *f*	French Riviera
côtelette *f*	cutlet
cotriade *f*	fish stew from Brittany
cou *m*	neck
couchette *f*	couchette ; bunk
couette *f*	continental quilt ; duvet
couler	to run *(water)*
couleur *f*	colour
coulis *m*	purée
couloir *m*	corridor
coulommiers *m*	cheese similar to camembert
coup *m*	stroke ; shot ; blow
coup de soleil	sunburn
coupe *f*	goblet ; dish ; scoop *(ice cream)*
coupe glacée	ice cream and fruit
couper	to cut
cour *f*	court ; courtyard
courant *m*	power ; current
courant(e)	common ; standard ; current
courge *f*	marrow *(vegetable)*
courrier *m*	mail ; post
courroie *f*	strap
cours *m*	lesson ; course ; rate
cours particuliers	private lessons

course f	**race** *(sport)* **; errand**
faire les courses	**to go shopping**
court(e)	**short**
court-bouillon m	**stock for poaching meat and fish**
couscous m	**spicy Arab dish of steamed semolina with a meat stew**
coût m	**cost**
couteau m	**knife**
coûteux (-euse)	**expensive**
couture f	**sewing**
couvent m	**convent ; monastery**
couvert m	**cover charge ; place setting**
couvert(e)	**covered**
couverture f	**blanket ; cover ; wrapper**
cravate f	**tie**
crayon m	**pencil**
crèche f	**day nursery**
crème f	**cream**
un (café) crème	**white coffee**
à la crème	**with cream**
crème anglaise	**custard**
crème caramel	**egg custard topped with caramel**
crème Chantilly	**whipped cream**
crème fouettée	**whipped cream**
crème pâtissière	**confectioner's custard**
crémerie f	**dairy**
crêpe f	**pancake**
crêpe fourrée	**stuffed pancake**
crêpe Suzette	**pancake served in flaming brandy**
crêperie f	**pancake shop/restaurant**
cresson m	**watercress**
crevette f	**shrimp**
crevette rose	**prawn**
croisière f	**cruise**
croix f	**cross**

croquant(e)	crisp ; crunchy
croque-madame m	toasted cheese sandwich with ham and fried egg
croque-monsieur m	toasted ham and cheese sandwich
croustade f	pastry shell with filling
croûte f	crust
en croûte	in a pastry crust
cru(e)	raw
premier cru	first-class wine
vin de grand cru	vintage wine
crudités fpl	raw vegetables
crustacés mpl	shellfish
cuiller f	spoon
cuiller à café	teaspoon
cuir m	leather
cuisine f	cooking ; cuisine ; kitchen
cuisine familiale	home cooking
cuisinier m	cook
cuisinière f	cook ; cooker
cuisse f	thigh
cuisses de grenouille	frogs' legs
cuit(e)	cooked ; done (steak)
cuivre m	copper
culturisme m	body-building
cuvée f	vintage
cylindrée f	(cubic) capacity (of engine)
d'abord	at first
d'accord	okay (agreement)
dacquoise f	meringue dessert
dactylo m/f	typist
daim m	suede
dames fpl	ladies' (toilets)

dans	into ; in ; on
danser	to dance
darne f	thick fish steak
date f	date (day)
datte f	date (fruit)
daube f	stew
daurade f	sea bream
de	from ; of
dé m	dice
en dés	diced
debout	standing ; upright
début m	beginning
débutant(e) m/f	beginner
décembre m	December
décès m	death
décharge f publique	rubbish dump
déchargement m	unloading
déci m	1 decilitre of wine (Switz.)
déclaration f	statement ; report
décollage m	takeoff
décolleté m	low neck
décongeler	to defrost
décontracté(e)	relaxed ; casual
décortiqué(e)	shelled
découverte f	discovery
décrocher	to lift the receiver (phone)
dédouaner	to clear customs
défaut m	fault ; defect
défectueux (-euse)	imperfect ; faulty
défense d'entrer	no entry
défense de stationner	no parking
dégâts mpl	damage
dégustation f	tasting

dehors	outside ; outdoors
déjeuner *m*	lunch ; breakfast *(Switz. only)*
petit déjeuner	breakfast
délit *m*	offence
demain	tomorrow
demande *f*	application
demandes d'emploi	situations wanted
demander	to ask (for)
démaquillant *m*	make-up remover
démarqué(e)	reduced *(goods)*
demi(e)	half
demi-pension *f*	half board
demi-sec	medium-dry
dent *f*	tooth
dentifrice *m*	toothpaste
dépannage *m*	breakdown
départ *m*	departure
département *m*	regional division *(France)*
dépasser	to exceed ; to overtake
dépenses *fpl*	expenditure ; outgoings
dépliant *m*	brochure
dépôt *m*	deposit ; depot
dépôt d'ordures	rubbish dump
depuis	since
déranger	to disturb
dernier (-ère)	last ; latest
derrière	at the back ; behind
dès	from ; since
dès votre arrivée	as soon as you arrive
descendre	to go down ; to get off *(bus)*
désirer	to want
désistement *m*	withdrawal
désodorisant *m*	air freshener
désolé(e)	sorry

dessin m	drawing
dessin animé	cartoon *(animated)*
dessous	underneath
dessus	on top
au dessus (de)	above
destinataire m/f	addressee
destination f	destination
à destination de	bound for
détail m : au détail	retail
prix de détail	retail price
détourner	to divert
deux	two
les deux	both
deuxième	second
deux-roues m	two-wheeled vehicle
devant	in front (of)
déviation f	diversion
devis m	quotation *(price)*
devises fpl	currency
dévisser	to unscrew
diapositive f	slide
diététique	dietary ; health foods
difficile	difficult
digue f	dyke ; jetty
dimanche m	Sunday
dinde f	turkey
dîner m	dinner ; dinner party ; lunch *(Switz.)*
dîner spectacle	cabaret dinner
direct(e): train direct	through train
directeur m	manager ; headmaster
direction f	management ; direction
toutes directions	through traffic ; all routes
directrice f	manageress ; headmistress
disponible	available

disque m	record ; disk
distractions fpl	entertainment
distributeur m	vending machine
divers(e)	various
docteur m	doctor
domicile m	home ; address
donner	to give ; to give away
doré(e)	golden
douane f	customs
doubler	to overtake
douce	gentle ; soft ; mild
douche f	shower
Douvres	Dover
doux	gentle ; soft ; mild
douzaine f	dozen
dragée f	sugared almond
drap m	sheet
droguerie f	hardware shop
droit m	right (entitlement)
droit(e)	right (not left) ; straight
droite f	right-hand side
à droite	on/to the right
dur(e)	hard ; hard-boiled
durée f	length (of time or stay)
eau f	water
eau gazeuse/plate	fizzy/still water
eau de Javel	bleach
eau du robinet	tap-water
eau-de-vie	brandy
échalote f	shallot
échantillon m	sample
éclairage m	lighting

écluse f	lock (in canal)
école f	school
écorce f	peel (of orange, lemon)
Ecosse f	Scotland
écossais(e)	Scottish
écouteur m	receiver
écran m	screen
écrevisse f	crayfish (freshwater)
écrire	to write
écurie f	stable
éditeur (-trice) m/f	publisher
églefin m	haddock
église f	church
élément m	unit ; element
emballage m	packing
embarquement m	boarding
embouteillage m	traffic jam
émincé m	thinly sliced meat in a sauce
émission f	programme ; broadcast
emmental m	Swiss cheese similar to gruyère
emploi m	use ; job
emporter	to take away
en	some ; any ; in ; to
en panne	out of order
en train/voiture	by train/ car
enceinte	pregnant
encore	still ; yet
encornet m	squid
endives fpl	chicory
endroit m	place ; spot
enfant m/f	child
enlever	to take away ; to remove
enneigement m	snowfall
ennui m	nuisance ; trouble

enregistrement m	check-in
enregistrer	to record ; to check in
enseignement m	education ; recording
ensemble	together
entier(ère)	whole
entracte m	interval
entre	between
entrecôte f	rib steak
entrecôte grillée	grilled rib steak
entrée f	entry ; admission ; starter (food)
prix d'entrée	admission fee
entrée gratuite	admission free
entrée interdite	no entry
entrepreneur m	contractor
entreprise f	firm ; company
entrer	to come in ; to go in
entretien m	maintenance ; interview
enveloppe f	envelope
envers m : l'envers	wrong side
à l'envers	upside down ; back to front
environ	around ; about
environs mpl	surroundings
épais(se)	thick
épargne f	saving
épaule f	shoulder
épi m	ear (of corn)
épi de maïs	corn-on-the-cob
épice f	spice
épicerie f	grocer's shop
épicerie fine	delicatessen
épilation f	hair removal
épinards mpl	spinach
épingle f	pin
éponge f	sponge

époque *f*	**age**
d'époque	**period** *(furniture)*
épreuve *f*	**event** *(sports)* ; **print** *(photographic)*
épuisé(e)	**sold out ; out of stock**
équipage *m*	**crew**
équipe *f*	**team ; shift**
équitation *f*	**horse-riding**
escalier *m*	**stairs**
escalier roulant	**escalator**
escalier de secours	**fire escape**
escalope *f*	**escalope**
escargot *m*	**snail**
espadon *m*	**swordfish**
Espagne *f*	**Spain**
espagnol(e)	**Spanish**
espèce *f*	**sort**
essai *m*	**trial ; test**
essayage *m*	**fitting** *(dress)*
essence *f*	**petrol**
essorer	**to spin(-dry) ; to wring**
est *m*	**east**
esthétique *f*	**beauty salon**
estivants *mpl*	**(summer) holiday-makers**
estomac *m*	**stomach**
estragon *m*	**tarragon**
crème d'estragon	**cream of tarragon (soup)**
esturgeon *m*	**sturgeon**
et	**and**
étage *m*	**storey**
premier étage	**first floor**
étain *m*	**tin ; pewter**
étang *m*	**pond**
étape *f*	**stage**
état *m*	**state**

été m	summer
éteindre	to turn off
éteignez vos phares	turn off your headlights
étoile f	star
étranger (-ère) m/f	foreigner
à l'étranger	overseas ; abroad
étroit(e)	narrow ; tight
étudiant(e) m/f	student
étudier	to study
étuvée f : à l'étuvée	braised
eux	them
événement m	occasion ; event
excursion f	trip ; outing ; excursion
excuses fpl	apologies
exemplaire m	copy
expéditeur m	sender
exportation f	export
exposition f	exhibition
exprès	on purpose ; deliberately
extérieur(e)	outside
extincteur m	fire extinguisher
extra	top-quality ; first-rate
fabrication f	manufacturing
fabriqué en ...	made in ...
face f : en face (de)	opposite
façon f	way ; manner
facture f	invoice
faïence f	earthenware
faim f	hunger
faire	to make ; to do
faites le 4	dial 4
faisan m	pheasant

French	English
fait(e): fait main	handmade
famille f	family
farce f	farce ; stuffing
farces et attrapes	jokes and novelties
farci(e)	stuffed
farine f	flour
fausse	fake ; false ; wrong
fauteuil m	armchair ; seat (at front of theatre)
faux	fake ; wrong ; false
faux-filet m	sirloin
félicitations fpl	congratulations
femme f	woman ; wife
femme de chambre	chambermaid
femme de ménage	cleaner (of house)
fenêtre f	window
fenouil m	fennel
fente f	crack, slot
fer m	iron (material, golf club)
féra f	freshwater fish (Switz.)
férié(e): jour férié	public holiday
ferme f	farmhouse ; farm
fermé(e)	shut
fermer	to close/shut ; to turn off (water)
fermer à clé	to lock
fermeture f	closing
fermier m	farmer
ferroviaire	railway ; rail
fête f	holiday ; fête
feu m	fire ; traffic lights
feu d'artifice	fireworks
feu rouge	red light
feuille f	sheet (of paper)
feuilleté(e)	made of puff pastry
feutre m	felt ; felt-tip pen

feux *mpl*	traffic lights
feux de position	sidelights
fève *f*	broad bean
fiche *f*	slip *(of paper)*
fièvre *f*	fever
figue *f*	fig
fil *m*	thread ; lead *(electrical)*
fil de fer	wire
file *f*	lane ; row *(behind one another)*
filet *m*	net ; fillet *(of meat, fish)*
filet à bagages	luggage rack
filet mignon	small steak
filets de perche	fried small fillets of perch
fille *f*	daughter ; girl
fils *m*	son
fin *f*	end
fin(e)	thin *(material)* ; fine *(delicate)*
fine *f* de claire	green oyster
fines herbes *fpl*	mixed herbs
finir	to end ; to finish
flacon *m*	bottle *(small)*
flamand(e)	Flemish
flambé(e)	flamed, usually with brandy
flan *m*	sweet or savoury tart
flétan *m*	halibut
fleur *f*	flower
fleuriste *m/f*	florist
fleuve *m*	river
flipper *m*	pinball
flocon *m*	flake
flocons d'avoine	rolled oats
flûte *f*	long, thin loaf
foie *m*	liver
foie gras	goose liver

foire f	fair
foire à/aux ...	special offer on ...
fois f	time
une fois	once
folle	mad
foncé(e)	dark (colour)
fonctionner	to work (machine)
fond m	back (of hall, room) ; bottom
fond d'artichaut	artichoke heart
fondue f	fondue
forêt f	forest
forfait m	fixed price ; ski pass
formel(le)	positive (definite)
formulaire m	form (document)
fou	crazy (prices)
fouettée	whipped (cream, eggs)
four m	oven
au four	baked
fourchette f	fork
fournir	to supply
fourré(e)	filled (pancake, etc.) ; fur-lined
fourrure f	fur
fraîche	fresh ; cool ; wet (paint)
frais	fresh ; cool
frais mpl	costs ; expenses
fraise f	strawberry
framboise f	raspberry
français(e)	French
frein m	brake
frère m	brother
fret m	freight (goods)
frisé(e)	curly
frisée f	curly endive
frit(e)	fried

213

frites *fpl*	French fried potatoes ; chips
friture *f*	fried food
froid(e)	cold
servir froid	serve chilled
fromage *m*	cheese
fromage blanc	soft white cheese
fromage frais	cream cheese
fromagerie *f*	cheese dairy
froment *m*	wheat
frontière *f*	border ; boundary
frotter	to rub
fruit *m*	fruit
fruits de mer	shellfish *(on menu)* ; seafood
fumer	to smoke
fumeur *m*	smoker
funiculaire *m*	funicular railway

galantine *f*	stuffed, pressed cold meat
galerie *f*	art gallery ; arcade *(commercial)*
galette *f*	flat cake
galette des rois	cake eaten on Twelfth Night
gambas *fpl*	large prawns
gant *m*	glove
garçon *m*	boy ; waiter
garde *m*	guard *(sentry)*
garder	to keep ; to look after
gardez vos distances	keep your distance
gardien(ne) *m/f*	caretaker ; warden
gare *f*	railway station
gare routière	bus terminal
garer	to park
garni(e)	served with vegetables
garni(e) frites	served with chips
gas-oil *m*	diesel fuel

gâteau *m*	cake ; gateau
gauche	left
à gauche	to/on the left
gaz *m*	gas
gazeux (-euse)	fizzy
gaz-oil *m*	diesel fuel
géant *m*	giant
gel *m*	frost
gelée *f*	jelly ; aspic
gendarme *m*	policeman
gendarmerie *f*	police station
génoise *f*	sponge cake
gérant(e) *m/f*	manager/manageress
Gewürztraminer *m*	fruity white wine from Alsace
gibier *m*	game *(hunting)*
gigot (d'agneau) *m*	leg of lamb
gingembre *m*	ginger
girolle *f*	chanterelle mushroom
gîte *m*	self-catering house/flat
glace *f*	ice ; ice cream ; mirror
glacé(e)	chilled ; iced
glacier *m*	glacier ; ice-cream maker
glaçon *m*	ice cube
glissant(e)	slippery
chaussée glissante	slippery road surface
gorge *f*	throat ; gorge
goût *m*	flavour ; taste
goûter	to taste
graine *f*	seed
graines de soja	soya beans
grand(e)	great ; high *(speed, number)* ; big
Grand Marnier *m*	orange liqueur
granité *m*	ice cream with crushed ice
gras(se)	fat ; greasy

gras-double *m*	tripe
gratin *m*	cheese-topped dish
au gratin	with cheese topping
gratin dauphinois	thinly-sliced potatoes baked with cream and gruyère cheese
gratiné(e)	with cheese topping
gratis	free
gratuit(e)	free of charge
gravure *f*	print *(picture)*
grec (grecque)	Greek
à la grecque	in olive oil and herbs
grenouille *f*	frog
grève *f*	strike *(industrial)*
grillade *f*	grilled meat
grille-pain *m*	toaster
gris(e)	grey
gros(se)	big *(sum of money)* ; large
en gros	in bulk ; wholesale
groseille *f*	redcurrant
groseille à maquereau	gooseberry
grotte *f*	cave
groupe *m*	group ; party
groupe sanguin	blood group
gruyère *m*	Swiss cheese with delicate flavour
guichet *m*	ticket office
guide *m/f*	guide
H	= heure
habitant(e) *m/f*	inhabitant
habituel(le)	usual ; regular
haché(e): steak haché	hamburger
hachis *m*	minced meat
hachis Parmentier	cottage pie
halles *fpl*	central food market

hareng *m*	herring
hareng saur	smoked herring
haricots *mpl*	beans
haricots blancs	haricot beans
haricots rouges	red kidney beans
haricots verts	green beans
haut *m*	top *(of ladder)*
haut(e)	high ; tall
hauteur *f*	height
hebdomadaire	weekly
hébergement *m*	lodging
herbe *f*: fines herbes	herbs
heure *f*	hour
à l'heure	on time
heureux (-euse)	happy
hier	yesterday
hippodrome *m*	racecourse
hiver *m*	winter
hollandais(e)	Dutch
sauce hollandaise	sauce made with butter, egg yolks and lemon juice
homard *m*	lobster
homard à la nage	lobster poached in stock
homard Thermidor	lobster cooked in cream and wine sauce
homme *m*	man
hôpital *m*	hospital
horaire *m*	timetable *(for trains, etc.)* ; schedule
horloge *f*	clock
hors: hors de	out of
hors service	out of order
hors d'œuvre *m*	starter
hors-saison	off-season
hors-taxe	duty-free

hôte *m*	host ; guest
hôtel *m*	hotel
hôtel de ville	town hall
huile *f*	oil *(edible, for car)*
huile d'arachide	groundnut oil
huile de tournesol	sunflower oil
huître *f*	oyster
hypermarché *m*	hypermarket
ici	here
il	he ; it
île *f*	island
île flottante	caramelized beaten egg white poached in milk, with almonds and floating in vanilla custard
illimité(e)	unlimited
immeuble *m*	block of flats
immobilier *m*	real estate
impair(e)	odd *(number)*
impasse *f*	dead end
imperméable	waterproof
impôt *m*	tax
imprimer	to print
incendie *m*	fire
inclu(e)	included ; inclusive
indicateur *m*	guide ; timetable
indicatif *m*	dialling code
indications *fpl*	instructions ; directions *(to a place)*
inférieur(e)	inferior ; lower
infirmerie *f*	infirmary
infirmier (-ière) *m/f*	nurse
informations *fpl*	news ; information
infusion *f*	herbal tea

inondation f	flood
inscrire	to write (down) ; to enrol
institut m	institute
institut de beauté	beauty salon
interdit(e)	forbidden
intéressant(e)	interesting
intérieur(e)	interior ; inside ; inner
introduire	to introduce ; to insert
inutile	useless ; unnecessary
invalide m/f	disabled person
invité(e) m/f	guest
issue f de secours	emergency exit
rue/voie sans issue	dead end ; no through road
italien(ne)	Italian
itinéraire m	route
itinéraire touristique	scenic route

jambon m	ham
jambon de Bayonne	cured Bayonne ham
jambon cuit	cooked ham
jambon cru	cured (raw) ham
jambon de Paris	boiled ham
jardin m	garden
jardin d'enfants	kindergarten
jardinière, à la	with selection of vegetables
jarret m	knuckle, shin (of veal, beef, etc.)
jaune	yellow
jetée f	pier
jeter	to throw
à jeter	disposable
jeu m	game ; set (collection) ; gambling
jeune	young
jeunesse f	youth
joindre	to join ; to enclose

joli(e)	pretty
jour *m*	day
journal *m*	newspaper
journée *f*	day *(length of time)*
juif (juive)	Jewish
julienne *f*	vegetables cut into fine strips
jumelé(e) avec ...	twinned with ...
jupe *f*	skirt
jus *m*	juice
jus de viande	gravy
jusqu'à	until ; till
kart *m*	go-cart
kas(c)her	kosher
kayac *m*	canoe
kilométrage *m*	= mileage
kilométrage illimité	unlimited mileage
kir *m*	dry white wine with splash of blackcurrant liqueur
klaxonner	to sound one's horn
kouglof/kugelhof *m*	type of cake from Alsace
lac *m*	lake
laine *f*	wool
laisse *f*	leash
laisser	to leave
laisser un message	leave a message
lait *m*	milk
lait démaquillant	cleansing milk
lait demi-écrémé	semi-skimmed milk
lait écrémé	skim(med) milk
lait entier	full-cream milk
laiterie *f*	dairy

laitue f	lettuce
lame f	blade
lampe f	light ; lamp
langouste f	crayfish (saltwater)
langoustines fpl	scampi
langue f	tongue ; language
lapin m	rabbit
lard m	fat ; (streaky) bacon
lard fumé	smoked bacon
lard maigre	lean bacon
lardon m	strip of fat
large	wide ; broad
largeur f	width
laurier m	sweet bay ; bay leaves
lavable	washable
lavabo m	washbasin
lavabos	toilets
lavage m	washing
lavande f	lavender
laverie automatique f	launderette
layette f	baby clothes
leçon f	lesson
leçons particulières	private lessons
léger(ère)	light (not heavy) ; weak (tea)
légumes mpl	vegetables
lentement	slowly
lentille f	lens (of glasses)
lentilles fpl	lentils
lessive f	soap powder ; washing
lettre f	letter
leur(s)	(to) them ; their
levain m	yeast
levée f	collection (of mail)
lever du soleil m	sunrise

221

levure f	yeast
librairie f	bookshop
libre	free ; vacant
libre-service	self-service
lieu m	place (location)
lièvre m	hare
ligne f	line ; service ; route (transport)
grandes lignes	main lines (trains)
limande-sole f	lemon sole
limitation f de vitesse	speed limit
limonade f	lemonade
lin m	linen (cloth)
linge m	linen (bed, table) ; laundry (clothes)
liste f	list
lit m	bed
grand lit	double bed
lit simple	single bed
lits jumeaux	twin beds
livarot m	pungent cheese from Normandy
livraison f	delivery (of goods)
livraison des bagages	baggage reclaim
livre f	pound
livre sterling	sterling
livre m	book
locataire m/f	tenant ; lodger
location f	rental ; hiring (out) ; letting
logement m	accommodation ; housing
loi f	law
loin	far
loisir m	leisure
long(ue)	long
le long de	along
longe f	loin (of meat)
longueur f	length

lot *m*	prize ; lot *(at auction)*
loto *m*	numerical lottery
lotte *f*	monkfish ; angler fish
louer	to let ; to hire ; to rent
loup *m*	wolf ; sea perch
loupe *f*	magnifying glass
lourd(e)	heavy
loyer *m*	rent
luge *f*	sledge ; toboggan
lumière *f*	light
lundi *m*	Monday
lune *f*	moon
lunettes *fpl*	glasses
lunettes de soleil	sunglasses
luxe *m*	luxury
lycée *m*	secondary school

M	sign for the Paris metro
macédoine *f* de fruits	fruit salad
Madame *f*	Mrs ; Ms ; Madam
madeleine *f*	small sponge cake
Mademoiselle *f*	Miss
madère *m*	Madeira *(wine)*
magasin *m*	shop
magnétophone *m*	tape recorder
magnétoscope *m*	video-cassette recorder
magret de canard *m*	breast fillet of duck
mai *m*	May
maigre	lean *(meat)*
maigrir	to slim
maillot de bain *m*	swimsuit
main *f*	hand
fait main	handmade

maintenant	now
mairie *f*	town hall
maïs *m*	maize
maïs doux	sweet corn
maison *f*	house ; home
maître d'hôtel *m*	head waiter
majuscule *f*	capital letter
mal *m*	harm ; pain
mal aux dents	toothache
le mal de mer	seasickness
mal de tête	headache
malade *m/f*	sick person ; patient
maladie *f*	disease
maman *f*	mummy
Manche (la)	the Channel
mandarine *f*	tangerine
mandat *m*	money order
manger	to eat
manifestation *f*	demonstration
manque *m*	shortage ; lack
par manque de ...	through lack of ...
manteau *m*	coat
maquereau *m*	mackerel
maquillage *m*	make-up
marbre *m*	marble *(material)*
marc *m*	white grape spirit
marchand *m*	dealer ; merchant
marchand de vin	wine merchant
marche *f*	step ; march
(en) marche	on *(machine)*
marche à pied	walking
marché *m*	market
marché aux puces	flea market
bon marché	inexpensive
marcher	to walk

mardi *m*	Tuesday
mardi gras	Shrove Tuesday
marée *f*	tide
marée basse/haute	low/high tide
marié *m*	bridegroom
Marie-Brizard ® *m*	aniseed-flavoured apéritif
mariée *f*	bride
mariné(e)	marinated
marionnettes *fpl*	puppets
marjolaine *f*	marjoram
marque *f*	make ; brand (name)
marron *m*	chestnut
marrons glacés	candied chestnuts
mars *m*	March
matériel *m*	equipment ; kit
matin *m*	morning
mauvais(e)	bad ; wrong
mazout *m*	oil *(for heating)*
médaillon *m*	thin, round slice of meat
médecin *m*	doctor
médicament *m*	medicine ; drug
meilleur(e)	best ; better
même	same
ménage *m*	housework
femme de ménage	cleaner
mensuel(le)	monthly
menthe *f*	mint ; mint tea
menu *m*	(set) menu
menu à prix fixe	set price menu
mer *f*	sea
mère *f*	mother
merlan *m*	whiting
mérou *m*	grouper
merveilleux (-euse)	wonderful ; marvellous

messe f	mass (church)
messieurs mpl	men ; gentlemen('s toilets)
mesure f	measurement
météo f	weather forecast
métier m	trade ; occupation ; craft
métro m	underground railway
mettre	to put ; to put on
meublé(e)	furnished
meubles mpl	furniture
meubles de style	period furniture
meunière	fish coated in flour and fried in butter with lemon juice
mi-bas mpl	knee socks
midi m	midday ; noon
le Midi	the south of France
miel m	honey
mieux	better ; best
milieu m	middle
millefeuille m	cream/vanilla slice
mince	slim ; thin
mine f	expression ; mine (for coal, etc.)
mineur(e)	under age ; minor (person)
mirabelle f	plum ; plum brandy
miroir m	mirror
mise en plis f	set (for hair)
mistral m	strong cold dry wind
mixte	mixed
mobilier m	furniture
mode f	fashion
mode d'emploi	instructions for use
moelle f	marrow (beef, etc.)
moins	minus ; less
le moins	the least
mois m	month

moitié f	half
à moitié	half
moka m	coffee cream cake ; mocha coffee
molle	soft
monde m	world ; people
moniteur m	instructor ; coach
monitrice f	instructress ; coach
monnaie f	currency ; change (money)
monnayeur m	automatic change machine
Monsieur m	Mr ; sir
monsieur	gentleman
montagne f	mountain
montant m	amount (total)
monter	to take up ; to go up ; to rise
montre f	watch
morceau m	piece ; bit ; cut (of meat)
Mornay, sauce	cheese sauce
mot m	note (letter) ; word
motif m	pattern
moto f	motorbike
mou	soft
mouche f	fly
mouchoir m	handkerchief
mouillé(e)	wet
moule f	mussel
moules marinières	mussels cooked in their shells with white wine and herbs
moulin m	mill
mousse f	foam ; mousse
mousse à raser	shaving foam
mousseux (-euse)	sparkling
moustique m	mosquito
moutarde f	mustard
mouton m	sheep ; lamb or mutton

moyenne f	average
muguet m	lily of the valley
muni(e) de	supplied with ; in possession of
munster m	strong cheese from Alsace
mur m	wall
mûr(e)	mature ; ripe
mûre f	blackberry
muscade f	nutmeg
muscat m	muscatel: a sweet dessert wine
musée m	museum ; art gallery
myrtille f	bilberry
nager	to swim
naissance f	birth
nappé(e)	coated (with chocolate, etc.)
natation f	swimming
naturel(le)	natural
au naturel	without seasoning or sweetening
nautique	nautical ; water-
navet m	turnip
navette f	shuttle (bus service)
navigation f	sailing
navire m	ship
ne/n': ne pas ...	do not ...
né(e)	born
nécessaire m	bag ; kit
neige f	snow
(à la) neige	with beaten egg-whites
nettoyage m	cleaning
nettoyage à sec	dry-cleaning
neuf	new
neuve	new
névralgie f	headache

nez *m*	nose
nid *m*	nest
niveau *m*	level ; standard
noce *f*	wedding
nocturne *m*	late opening
match en nocturne	floodlit fixture
Noël *m*	Christmas
noir(e) *f*	black
noisette *f*	hazelnut
noisette d'agneau	small boneless slice of lamb
noix *f*	walnut
noix de muscade	nutmeg
nom *m*	name
nom de famille	surname
nom de jeune fille	maiden name
nombre *m*	number
non	no ; not
non-fumeur *m*	non-smoker
nord *m*	north
normal(e)	normal ; standard *(size)* ; regular
notaire *m*	solicitor
note *f*	note ; bill ; memo
nougatine *f*	sponge cake with praline cream
nouilles *fpl*	noodles
nourriture *f*	food
nouveau	new
Nouvel An *m*	New Year
nouvelle	new
nouvelles *fpl*	news
novembre *m*	November
noyer *m*	walnut
nu(e)	naked ; bare
nuit *f*	night
numéro *m*	number ; act ; issue *(of magazine)*

objectif *m*	objective ; lens *(of camera)*
objet *m*	object
objets de valeur	valuable items
objets trouvés	lost property
obligatoire	compulsory
occasion *f*	occasion ; bargain
d'occasion	used ; second-hand
occupé(e)	engaged ; busy ; hired *(taxi)*
octobre *m*	October
œuf *m*	egg
œufs brouillés	scrambled eggs
œuf à la coque	soft-boiled egg
œuf dur	hard-boiled egg
œuf sur le plat	fried egg
œuf poché	poached egg
office *m* du tourisme	tourist office
offre *f*	offer
oie *f*	goose
oignon *m*	onion
oiseau *m*	bird
olive *f*	olive
olivier *m*	olive (tree) ; olive *(wood)*
omelette *f*	omelette
omelette baveuse	runny omelette
onde *f*	wave
or *m*	gold
orage *m*	thunderstorm
orange *f*	orange
orange pressée	fresh orange drink
ordinaire	ordinary
(essence) ordinaire	= 2-star petrol
ordonnance *f*	prescription
ordre *m*	order
à l'ordre de	payable to
ordures *fpl*	rubbish

oreille f	ear
orgeat m	barley
os m	bone
oseille f	sorrel
osier m	wicker
ou	or
où	where
oursin m	sea urchin
ouvert(e)	open ; on *(water, gas, etc.)*
ouverture f	overture ; opening
ouvrable	working *(day)*

paiement m	payment
paille f	straw
pain m	bread ; loaf of bread
petit pain	roll
pain bis	brown bread
pain au chocolat	croissant with chocolate filling
pain complet	wholemeal bread
pain grillé	toast
pain de mie	sandwich loaf
pain de seigle	rye bread
pair(e)	even
paire f	pair
palais m	palace
palourde f	clam
pamplemousse m	grapefruit
panaché m	shandy
pané(e)	in breadcrumbs
panier m	basket
panier repas	packed lunch
panne f	breakdown
en panne	out of order
panneau m	sign

pantalon m	trousers
papeterie f	stationer's shop
papier m	paper
papiers	identity papers ; driving licence
papier hygiénique	toilet paper
Pâques m or fpl	Easter
paquet m	package ; pack ; packet
par	by ; through ; per
deux fois par jour	twice a day
parapluie m	umbrella
parc m	park
parc d'attractions	amusement park
parcmètre m	parking meter
pare-brise m	windscreen
parent(e) m/f	relative
parfait m	ice cream dessert with fruit
parfait(e)	perfect
parfum m	perfume ; flavour
parfumerie f	perfume shop
parking souterrain	underground car park
parking surveillé	attended car park
parler	to speak ; to talk
Parmentier	see hachis
paroisse f	parish
parterre m	flowerbed
partie f	part ; round (in competition)
partir	to leave ; to go
à partir de	from
pas	not
pas m	step ; pace
passage m	passage
passage clouté	pedestrian crossing
passage interdit	no through way
passage à niveau	level crossing
passage souterrain	underpass (for pedestrians)

passager (-ère) *m/f*	**passenger**
passé(e)	**past**
passer	**to pass ; to spend** *(time)*
se passer	**to happen**
passerelle *f*	**gangway** *(bridge)*
passionnant(e)	**exciting**
pastèque *f*	**watermelon**
pasteur *m*	**minister** *(of religion)*
pastis *m*	**aniseed-flavoured apéritif**
pâte *f*	**pastry ; dough ; paste ; batter**
pâté *m*	**pâté**
pâté en croûte	**pâté in a pastry crust**
patère *f*	**peg** *(for coat)*
pâtes *fpl*	**pasta**
patin *m*	**skate**
patins à glace	**ice skates**
patins à roulettes	**roller skates**
patinoire *f*	**skating rink**
pâtisserie *f*	**cake shop ; pastry** *(cake)*
pâtissier-glacier *m*	**confectioner and ice-cream maker**
patron *m*	**boss ; pattern** *(dressmaking, knitting)*
patronne *f*	**boss**
paupiettes de veau *fpl*	**veal olives**
payé(e)	**paid**
payé(e) d'avance	**prepaid**
payer	**to pay (for)**
pays *m*	**land ; country**
du pays	**local**
paysage *m*	**scenery**
Pays-Bas *mpl*	**Netherlands**
péage *m*	**toll** *(motorway, etc.)*
peau *f*	**hide** *(leather)* **; skin**
pêche *f*	**peach ; fishing**
pêcheur *m*	**angler**

pédicure *m/f*	chiropodist
peignoir *m*	dressing gown ; bathrobe
peindre	to paint ; to decorate
peinture *f*	paint
pellicule *f*	film *(for camera)*
pelote *f*	ball *(of string, wool)*
pelote basque	pelota *(ball game for 2 players)*
pelouse *f*	lawn
pencher	to lean
se pencher	to lean out
pendant	during
penser	to think
pension *f*	guesthouse
demi-pension	half board
pension complète	full board
pente *f*	slope
Pentecôte *f*	Whitsun
perche *f*	perch
perdre	to lose
perdrix *f*	partridge
père *m*	father
périmé(e)	out of date
périphérique *m*	ring road
perle *f*	bead ; pearl
permettre	to permit *(something)*
permis *m*	permit
permis de conduire	driving licence
Pernod ® *m*	aniseed-based apéritif
persil *m*	parsley
pétanque *f*	type of bowls
pétillant(e)	fizzy
petit(e)	small ; slight
petit déjeuner	breakfast
petits pois	(garden) peas

petit-beurre m	butter biscuit
petite friture f	whitebait
petit-suisse m	fresh unsalted double-cream cheese, eaten with sugar or fruit
pétrole m	oil (petroleum) ; paraffin
peu	little
phare m	headlight ; lighthouse
pharmacie f	chemist's (shop) ; pharmacy
pichet m	jug
pièce f	room (in house) ; coin
pièce d'identité	(means of) identification
pièce de rechange	spare part
pied m	foot
à pied	on foot
pierre f	stone
piéton m	pedestrian
pignon m	pine kernel
pile f	pile ; battery (for radio, etc.)
pilon m	drumstick (of chicken)
pilule f	pill
piment m	chili
pintade(au) f	guinea fowl
pipérade f	lightly scrambled eggs with tomato and peppers
piquant(e)	spicy ; hot
piqûre f	bite (by insect) ; injection ; sting
piscine f	swimming pool
pissaladière f	onion tart with black olives and anchovies
pissenlit m	dandelion
pistache f	pistachio (nut)
piste f	ski run
piste pour débutants	nursery slope
piste de luge	toboggan run
pistes tous niveaux	slopes for all levels of skiers

place f	**square** (in town) **; seat ; space** (room)
sur place	on the spot
places debout	standing room
plage f	beach
plaisir m	enjoyment ; pleasure
plan m	map (of town)
planche f	plank
planche à voile	windsurfing
plaque f minéralogique	number plate
plat m	dish ; course (of meal)
plat du jour	dish of the day
plat de résistance	main course
plats à emporter	take-away meals
plat(e)	level (surface) ; flat
plateau m	tray
plein(e)	full
plein(e) de	full of
plein sud	facing south
plomb m	lead
essence sans plomb	unleaded petrol
plombier m	plumber
plombières f	tutti-frutti ice cream with cream
plonger	to dive
pluie f	rain
plus	more ; most
pneu m	tyre
poche f	pocket
poché(e)	poached
poids m	weight
poids lourd	heavy goods vehicle
poil m	hair ; coat (of animal)
poinçonner	to punch (ticket, etc.)
point m	stitch ; dot
à point	medium (steak)
point de rencontre	meeting point

pointure f	**size** (of shoes)
poire f	**pear ; pear brandy**
poire belle Hélène	**poached pear served with vanilla ice cream and hot chocolate sauce**
poireau m	**leek**
pois m	**spot** (dot)
petits pois	**peas**
pois cassés	**split peas**
pois chiches	**chick peas**
poisson m	**fish**
poisson rouge	**goldfish**
poissonnerie f	**fishmonger's shop**
poitrine f	**breast ; chest**
poivre m	**pepper**
poivron m	**pepper** (capsicum)
police f	**policy** (insurance) **; police**
police secours	**emergency services**
policier m	**policeman ; detective film/novel**
pomme f	**apple ; potato**
pommes à l'anglaise	**boiled potatoes**
pommes (au) four	**baked potatoes**
pommes frites	**chips**
pommes sautées	**sautéed potatoes**
pommes vapeur	**boiled potatoes**
pomme de terre f	**potato**
pommes de terre en robe des champs	**jacket potatoes**
pommier m	**apple tree**
pompes funèbres fpl	**undertaker's**
pompier m	**fireman**
pont m	**bridge ; deck** (of ship)
faire le pont	**to have long holiday weekend**
pont-l'évêque m	**mature, square-shaped cheese**
porc m	**pork ; pig**
port m	**harbour ; port**
porte f	**door ; gate**

porteur m	porter
portier m	doorman
portion f	helping ; portion
porto m	port (wine)
port-salut m	mild firm cheese
poser	to put ; to lay down
posologie f	dosage
posséder	to own
poste m	(radio/TV) set ; extension (phone)
poste de contrôle	checkpoint
poste de secours	first-aid post
poste f	post
pot m	pot (jam, plant) ; carton (yoghurt, etc.)
potable: eau potable	drinking water
potage m	soup
pot-au-feu m	beef stew
poteau m	post (pole)
poteau indicateur	signpost
potée f	pork or beef hotpot
potiron m	pumpkin
poubelle f	dustbin
poudre f	powder
poule f	hen
poule en daube	chicken casserole
poule au pot	stewed chicken with vegetables
poulet m	chicken
poulet en cocotte	chicken casserole
poulet frites	chicken with chips
poulet rôti	roast chicken
pourboire m	tip
pourquoi	why
pousser	to push
pousses de soja fpl	beansprouts
pouvoir	to be able
praire f	clam

praline f	sugared almond
préfecture de police f	police headquarters
premier(ère)	first
premiers secours	first aid
prendre	to take ; to get ; to catch
prénom m	first name
près (de)	near
présenter	to present ; to introduce
pressé(e)	squeezed ; pressed
pressing m	dry cleaner's
pression f	pressure
(bière à la) pression	draught beer
prêt(e)	ready
prêt à cuire	ready to cook
prêt-à-porter m	ready-to-wear
prévision f	forecast
prière de ...	please ...
printemps m	spring
priorité f	right of way
cédez la priorité	give way
priorité à droite	give way to traffic from right
prise f	plug ; socket
privé(e)	private
prix m	price ; prize
à prix réduit	cut-price
prix du billet	fare
prochain(e)	next
proche	close (near)
produits mpl	produce ; products
profiter de	to take advantage of
profiteroles fpl	choux-pastry balls filled with cream
profond(e)	deep
profondeur f	depth
promenade f	walk ; promenade ; ride (in vehicle)

promotionnel(le)	special low-price
propre	clean ; own
propriétaire *m/f*	owner
propriété *f*	property
provenance *f*	origin ; source
en provenance de ...	coming from ...
provençal(e)	cooked in olive oil, with tomatoes, garlic and parsley
provisions *fpl*	groceries
provisoirement	for the time being
prune *f*	plum ; plum brandy
pruneau *m*	prune ; damson (Switz.)
pruneau sec	prune (Switz.)
P.T.T. *fpl*	Post Office
puce *f*	flea
(marché aux) puces	flea market
puissance *f*	power
puits *m*	well (for water)
purée *f*	purée ; mashed
P.V. *m*	parking ticket

quai *m*	platform (in station) ; wharf ; quay
quand	when
quarantaine *f*	about forty ; quarantine
quartier *m*	neighbourhood ; district
que	that ; than ; whom ; what
quel(le)	which ; what
quelque	some
quelque chose	something
quelqu'un	someone
quenelle *f*	light fish/poultry/meat dumpling
quetsche *f*	damson ; damson brandy
queue *f*	queue ; tail

qui	who ; which
quincaillerie f	hardware
quinzaine f	about fifteen ; a fortnight
quotidien(ne)	daily
rabais m	reduction
raccrocher	to hang up (phone)
raclette f	hot, melted cheese served with boiled potatoes and pickles
radis m	radish
rafraîchissements mpl	refreshments
rage f	rabies
ragoût m	stew ; casserole
raie f	skate (fish)
raifort m	horseradish
raisin m	grape
raisin sec	sultana ; raisin
raisins de mars	redcurrants (Switz. only)
raison f	reason
ralentir	to slow down
randonnée f	hike
râpé(e)	grated
rapide	quick ; fast
rapide m	express train
raquette f	racket (tennis) ; bat ; snowshoe
rare	rare ; unusual
rascasse f	scorpion fish
rasoir m	razor
ratatouille (niçoise) f	aubergines, peppers, courgettes and tomatoes cooked in olive oil
R.A.T.P. f	Paris transport authority
rayon m	shelf ; department (in store)
rayon hommes	menswear (department)

R. de C./RC.	*see* **rez-de-chaussée**
reboucher	to recork
recette *f*	recipe
recharge *f*	refill
rechargeable	refillable *(lighter, pen)*
réclamation *f*	complaint
réclame *f*	advertisement
recommandé(e)	registered *(mail)*
récompense *f*	reward
reçu *m*	receipt
réduction *f*	reduction ; discount
refuge *m*	mountain hut
refuser	to reject ; to refuse
régime *m*	diet *(slimming)*
règlement *m*	regulation ; payment
régler	to pay ; to settle
réglisse *f*	liquorice
reine *f*	queen
relais routier *m*	transport café (good value food)
rembourser	to pay back ; to refund
remède *m*	remedy
remercier	to thank
remorquer	to tow
rémoulade *f*	mayonnaise with onions, capers, gherkins and herbs
remplir	to fill ; to fill in/out/up
rencontrer	to meet
rendez-vous *m*	date ; appointment
rendre	to give back
renouveler	to renew
renseignements *mpl*	information ; directory enquiries
rentrée *f*	return to work after break
rentrée (des classes)	start of the new school year

réparations *fpl*	**repairs**
repas *m*	**meal**
repasser	**to iron**
répondre	**to reply ; to answer**
réponse *f*	**answer ; reply**
repos *m*	**rest**
représentation *f*	**performance** (of play)
requis(e)	**required**
R.E.R. *m*	**Paris high-speed commuter train**
réseau *m*	**network**
réservation *f*	**reservation ; booking**
rester	**to remain ; to stay**
restoroute *m*	**roadside or motorway restaurant**
retard *m*	**delay**
en retard	**late**
retirer	**to withdraw ; to collect** (tickets)
retour *m*	**return** (going/coming back)
retrait *m*	**withdrawal ; collection**
retrait d'espèces	**cash withdrawal**
retraité(e) *m/f*	**old-age-pensioner**
réunion *f*	**meeting**
réveil *m*	**alarm clock**
réveillon *m*	**Christmas/New Year's Eve**
rez-de-chaussée *m*	**ground floor**
rien	**nothing ; anything**
rillettes *fpl*	**potted meat, pork or goose**
ris de veau *m*	**calf sweetbread**
rivière *f*	**river**
riz *m*	**rice**
riz au lait	**rice pudding**
R.N.	*see* route
robe *f*	**gown ; dress**
robinet *m*	**tap**
rocade *f*	**ringroad**

rocher m	**rock** (boulder)
rognon m	**kidney** (to eat)
roi m	**king**
la fête des rois	Twelfth Night ; Epiphany
romaine f	**cos lettuce**
roman m	**novel**
Romandie f	**French speaking Switzerland**
romarin m	**rosemary**
romsteak m	**rump steak**
rond(e)	**round**
roquefort m	**rich, pungent blue-veined cheese**
rosbif m	**roast beef ; roasting beef**
rose	**pink**
rôti m	**roast meat ; joint**
rôtisserie f	**steakhouse ; roast meat counter**
roue f	**wheel**
rouge	**red**
rouget m	**mullet**
rouille f	**spicy hot sauce for fish**
roulade f	**rolled meat or fish with stuffing**
rouler	**to roll ; to go** (by car)
roulez lentement	drive slowly
route f	**road ; route**
route barrée	road closed
route nationale	trunk-road
routier m	**lorry driver**
Royaume-Uni m	**United Kingdom**
rue f	**street**
ruelle f	**lane** (in town) **; alley**
rumsteck m	**rump steak**
russe	**Russian**
rutabaga m	**swede**

S.A.	Ltd ; plc
sabayon *m*	egg-yolk dessert served warm
sable *m*	sand
sables mouvants	quicksand
sablé *m*	shortbread
sac *m*	bag
sac à dos	rucksack
sachet *m*	sachet
sachet de thé	tea bag
safran *m*	saffron
sage	good *(well-behaved)* ; wise
saignant(e)	rare *(steak)*
saint(e) *m/f*	saint
saint-honoré *m*	gateau decorated with whipped cream and choux pastry balls
saint-nectaire *m*	firm fruity-flavoured cheese
saint-paulin *m*	mild cow's-milk cheese
Saint-Sylvestre *f*	New Year's Eve
saison *f*	season
haute/basse saison	high/low season
salade *f*	lettuce ; salad
salade lyonnaise	potato, sausage and gherkin salad
salade niçoise	French bean, tomato, pepper, potato, olive and anchovy salad
salaisons *fpl*	salt meats
sale	dirty
salé(e)	salty ; savoury
salle *f*	lounge *(at airport)* ; hall *(room)*
salle d'attente	waiting room
salle à manger	dining room
salon *m*	sitting room ; lounge ; salon
samedi *m*	Saturday
sanglier *m*	wild boar
sans	without
sans issue	no through road

santé f	health
sapin m	fir (tree)
S.A.R.L. f	limited company
sarriette f	savory (herb)
sauce f	sauce
saucisse f	sausage
saucisson m	type of salami
sauf	except (for)
sauge f	sage (herb)
saumon m	salmon
saumon fumé	smoked salmon
sauté(e)	fried in olive oil or butter
savarin m	cake soaked in syrup and liqueur
savon m	soap
scarole f	endive
scotch m	Sellotape ® ; whisky
séance f	meeting ; performance
sec (sèche)	dried (fruit, beans)
sèche-cheveux m	hairdryer
secouer	to shake
secours m	help
secrétariat m	office
secteur m	sector ; mains
sécurité f	security ; safety
séjour m	stay ; visit
sel m	salt
self m	self-service restaurant
semaine f	week
semoule f	semolina
sens m	meaning ; direction
sens interdit	no entry
sens unique	one-way street
sentier m	footpath
série f	series ; set

serrer	to grip ; to squeeze
véhicules lents	slow-moving vehicles keep to the
serrez à droite	right-hand lane
serrurerie f	locksmith's
servez-vous	help yourself
service m	service ; service charge
service compris	service included
serviette f	towel ; serviette ; briefcase
servir	to dish up ; to serve
seul(e)	alone ; lonely
seulement	only
si	if ; yes (to negative question)
siècle m	century
siège m	seat ; head office
siège social	registered office
signal m	signal
signaler	to report
simple	simple ; single
sirop m	syrup
site m	site
site touristique	tourist spot
situé(e)	located
ski m	ski ; skiing
slip m	underpants ; panties
snack m	snack bar
S.N.C.F. f	French railways
société f	company ; society
sœur f	sister
soie f	silk
soif f	thirst
soin m	care
aux bons soins de	care of (c/o)
soir m	evening
ce soir	tonight

soirée f	evening ; party
soja m	soya ; soya beans
germes de soja	beansprouts
sol m	ground ; soil
solde m	balance (remainder owed)
soldes mpl	sales (cheap prices)
soldes permanents	sale prices all year round
sole f	sole (fish)
soleil m	sun ; sunshine
sommelier m	wine waiter
sonner	to ring ; to strike
sorbet m	water ice
sortie f	exit
sortie interdite	no exit
sortie de secours	emergency exit
souhaiter	to wish
soulever	to lift
soupe f	soup
soupe au chou	cabbage soup
soupe à l'oignon	onion soup
soupe au pistou	thick bean and vegetable soup
sourd(e)	deaf
sous	underneath ; under
sous-sol m	basement
sous-vêtements mpl	underwear ; underclothes
souterrain(e)	underground
soutien-gorge m	bra
spectacle m	show (in theatre) ; entertainment
spectateurs mpl	audience (in theatre)
spiritueux mpl	spirits
sportif (-ive)	sports ; athletic
S.S. (sous-sol)	basement
stade m	stadium
standard m	switchboard

standardiste *m/f*	switchboard operator
station *f*	station (metro) ; resort
station balnéaire	seaside resort
station climatique	health resort
station de taxis	taxi rank
station thermale	spa
stationnement *m*	parking
steak *m*	steak
steak au poivre	steak with peppercorns
steak tartare	minced raw steak with raw egg, onion, tartar sauce and parsley
stylo *m*	pen ; fountain pen
sucette *f*	lollipop
sucre *m*	sugar
sucre glace	icing sugar
sucre roux	brown sugar
sucré(e)	sweet
sud *m*	south
suisse	Swiss
Suisse *f*	Switzerland
suite *f*	series ; continuation
suivant(e)	following
suivre	to follow
faire suivre	please forward (letter)
super(carburant) *m*	four-star petrol
supplément *m*	extra charge
supplémentaire	extra
suprême *m* de volaille	chicken breast in creamy sauce
sur	on ; onto ; on top of ; upon
3 mètres sur 5	3 metres by 5
surgelés *mpl*	frozen foods
surveillé(e)	supervised
s.v.p.	please
sympa(thique)	nice ; pleasant
syndicat d'initiative *m*	tourist office

ta	**your** *(familiar form)*
tabac *m*	**tobacco ; tobacconist's**
table *f*	**table**
table d'hôte	**fixed-price menu**
tableau *m*	**painting ; picture ; board**
taille *f*	**size** *(of clothes)* **; waist**
grande taille	**outsize** *(clothes)*
taille unique	**one size**
tailleur *m*	**tailor ; suit** *(women's)*
talon *m*	**heel ; stub** *(counterfoil)*
talon minute	**shoes reheeled while you wait**
tante *f*	**aunt**
taper	**to strike ; to type**
tapis *m*	**carpet**
tard	**late**
au plus tard	**at the latest**
tarif *m*	**rate ; tariff**
tarte *f*	**flan ; tart**
tarte au citron	**lemon tart**
tarte Tatin	**upside-down apple tart**
tartine *f*	**slice of bread and butter (or jam)**
tartiner: à tartiner	**for spreading**
tasse *f*	**cup ; mug**
taux *m*	**rate**
taux fixe	**flat rate**
taxe *f*	**duty ; tax** *(on goods)*
T.C.F.	**Touring Club de France** *(automobile)*
teint *m*	**complexion**
teinturerie *f*	**dry cleaner's**
télé *f*	**TV**
télébenne *f*	**gondola lift**
télécabine *f*	**gondola lift**
télécarte *f*	**phonecard**
téléphérique *m*	**cableway ; cable-car**
télésiège *m*	**chair-lift**

téléviseur *m*	television *(set)*
tempête *f*	storm
temps *m*	weather ; time
tenir	to hold ; to keep
tenez votre droite	keep to the right
tennis *m*	tennis
tension *f*	voltage
tente *f*	tent
tenue *f*	clothes ; dress
tenue de soirée	evening dress
terrain *m*	ground ; land ; pitch ; course *(golf)*
terrasse *f*	terrace
terre *f*	land ; earth ; ground
terrine *f*	terrine ; pâté
tête *f*	head
T.G.V. *m*	high-speed train
thé *m*	tea
thé au citron	lemon tea
thé au lait	tea with milk
thé nature	tea without milk
théière *f*	teapot
thon *m*	tuna(-fish)
ticket *m*	ticket *(for bus, metro)*
ticket de caisse	receipt
tiède	lukewarm
tiers *m*	third party
tilleul *m*	lime (tree) ; lime tea
timbale *f*	pastry mould
timbre *m*	stamp
tirage *m*	printing ; print *(photo)*
tirage le mercredi	lottery draw on Wednesdays
tirez	pull
tisane *f*	herbal tea
tissu *m*	material ; fabric

titre m	title
à titre indicatif	for information only
à titre provisoire	provisionally
titulaire m/f	holder of (card, etc.)
toboggan m	flyover (road) ; slide (chute)
toile f	canvas
toilettes fpl	toilet ; powder room
tomate f	tomato
tomme (de Savoie) f	mild soft cheese
tonalité f	dialling tone
tordre	to twist
tôt	early
toujours	always ; still
tour f	tower
tour m	trip ; walk ; ride
touriste m/f	tourist (person)
touristique	tourist (route, resort, etc.)
tournedos m	thick slice of beef fillet
tournedos Rossini	beef fillet with foie gras, truffles, in Madeira wine sauce
tourte f	pie
tous	all (plural)
Toussaint f	All Saints' Day
tout(e)	all ; everything
tout droit	straight ahead
toute la journée	all day
toutes	all (plural)
toutes directions	all routes
tout le monde	everyone
toux f	cough
train m	train
trajet m	journey
tranche f	slice
transférer	to transfer

travail *m*	work
travaux *mpl*	road works
traversée *f*	crossing *(voyage)*
très	very ; much
tricot *m*	knitting ; sweater
trimestre *m*	term
tripes *fpl*	tripe
troisième	third
du troisième âge	senior citizen
trop	too
trottoir *m*	pavement
trouver	to find
se trouver	to be (situated)
truffe *f*	truffle
truite *f*	trout
truite au bleu	boiled fresh trout
T.V.A. *f*	V.A.T.
ultérieur(e)	later *(date, etc.)*
un(e)	one ; a ; an
uni(e)	plain *(not patterned)*
uniquement	only
urgence *f*	urgency ; emergency
usage *m*	use
usine *f*	factory
vacances *fpl*	holiday(s)
grandes vacances	summer holidays
vache *f*	cow
vacherin glacé *m*	ice cream in a meringue shell
vaisselle *f*	crockery
valider	to validate

valise f	suitcase
vapeur f	steam
vaporisateur m	spray (container)
varié(e)	varied ; various
veau m	calf ; veal
végétal(e)	vegetable
véhicule m	vehicle
vélo m	bike
velouté m	classic cream sauce made with white wine ; creamy soup
vendange(s) f(pl)	harvest (of grapes)
vendeur (-euse) m/f	sales assistant
vendre	to sell
vendredi m	Friday
le vendredi saint	Good Friday
venir	to come
vente f	sale
date limite de vente	sell-by date
vente aux enchères	auction
verglacé(e)	icy
verglas m	black ice
vérification f	check(ing)
vérifier	to audit ; to check
verre m	glass
verres de contact	contact lenses
vers	toward(s) ; about
versement m	payment ; instalment
vert(e)	green
verveine f	verbena ; verbena tea
veste f	jacket
vestiaire m	cloakroom
vêtements mpl	clothes
vétérinaire m/f	vet
veuillez...	please...

viande *f*	meat
viande séchée	thin slices of cured beef
vichyssoise *f*	cream of leek and potato soup
vidange *f*	oil change *(car)*
vide	empty
vie *f*	life
à vie	for life
vieille	old
vieux	old
vigne *f*	vine ; vineyard
ville *f*	town
vin *m*	wine
vin du cru	locally grown wine
vin de pays	good but not top-class wine
vinaigrette *f*	vinaigrette ; salad dressing
virage *m*	bend *(in road)* ; curve ; corner
visage *m*	face
visite *f*	visit ; consultation *(of doctor)*
visite guidée	guided tour
visser	to screw
vite	quickly ; fast
vitesse *f*	gear *(of car)* ; speed
vitesse limitée à ...	speed limit ...
vitre *f*	pane ; window *(in car, train)*
vitrine *f*	shop window
vivre	to live
vœu *m*	wish
meilleurs vœux	best wishes
voici	here is/are
voie *f*	lane *(of road)* ; line ; track *(for trains)*
voie de droite	inside lane
voie de gauche	outside lane
voilà	there is/are
voisin(e) *m/f*	neighbour
voiture *f*	car ; coach *(of train)*

vol *m*	flight ; theft
volaille *f*	poultry
voleur *m*	thief
volonté *f*	will
à volonté	as much as you like *(wine, etc.)*
vos	your *(polite, plural form)*
v.o.s.t.	original version with subtitles *(film)*
votre	your *(polite, plural form)*
vous	you ; to you *(polite, plural form)*
voyage *m*	journey
voyage organisé	package holiday
voyageur *m*	traveller
vrai(e)	real ; true
vue *f*	view ; sight
wagon *m*	carriage ; waggon
wagon-couchettes *m*	sleeping car
wagon-restaurant *m*	dining car
w-c *mpl*	toilet
xérès *m*	sherry
y	there ; on it ; in it
yaourt *m*	yoghurt
yeux *mpl*	eyes
zone *f*	zone
zone piétonne	pedestrian precinct